ZIMBOLICIOUS ANTHOLOGY:

An Anthology of Zimbabwean Literature and Arts

VOLUME 5

Edited by Tendai R Mwanaka

Mwanaka Media and Publishing Pvt Ltd,
Chitungwiza Zimbabwe
*
Creativity, Wisdom and Beauty

Publisher: Mmap
Mwanaka Media and Publishing Pvt Ltd
24 Svosve Road, Zengeza 1
Chitungwiza Zimbabwe
mwanaka@yahoo.com
www.africanbookscollective.com/publishers/mwanaka-media-and-publishing
https://facebook.com/MwanakaMediaAndPublishing/

Distributed in and outside N. America by African Books Collective
orders@africanbookscollective.com
www.africanbookscollective.com

ISBN: 978-1-77929-609-2
EAN: 978177929-6092

DISCLAIMER
All views expressed in this publication are those of the author and do not necessarily
reflect the views of *Mmap*.

iii

About the editor

Tendai Rinos Mwanaka is a Zimbabwean publisher, editor, mentor, thinker, literary artist, visual artist and musical artist with over 30 books published. He writes in English and Shona. His work has been nominated, shortlisted and won several prizes, that has also appeared in over 400 journals and anthologies from over 30 countries, and translated into Spanish, Serbian, Arabic, Bengali, Tamil, Macedonian, Albanian, Hungarian, Russian, Romanian, French and German.

Table of Contents

vii

Contributor's Bio Notes

My name is **Tinashe Trymore Munengwa**. I was born in Bulawayo and attended Gifford High school where I did my form 1 to 6. My rural home is in Chivhu. I hold a Bachelor of Arts Degree and Post Graduate Diploma in Education. I have taught English and Geography at various government and private school including Gifford in Bulawayo as well as Liebenberg High School and Unyetu Secondary School both in Chivhu. I live in Chitungwiza where I teach Literature in English and Communication Skills at Lyndel House College

. **Matthew K Chikono** is a storyteller from Chitungwiza, Zimbabwe. His short fiction has appeared in Zimbolicious Anthology volume 4, Boys Are Not Stones Anthology volume 2 and The World of Myth May 2020 issue. He is also the co-writer of the Themba, a Ndebele superhero comic book series.

My name is **Everjoice Marwa**. I am Lady aged 27 and currently studying Bachelor of Education Honours Degree at Great Zimbabwe University majoring in English and History. I am still in my first year. I was born and bred in Chipinge and l was married in Nyanga. I did my high school level at Mutema high school in Chipinge. I enjoy writing as a hobby. I usually write poetry or prose. Below are my contact details followed by the two poems that l have written. I would be very happy to get your feedback after reading them and it will be a bonus if they get to be published.

Zvikomborero Kapuya is the author of Phenomenology of Decolonizing The University: Contemporary Thoughts in Afrikology

Prince Michael Zimbango, working under the pseudonym **Michael Perseus,** is a Biochemistry student with deep ties to poetry who wishes to share his work with the world around and help build greater awareness and visibility for the poetry community. He can be found on Instagram @michael_perseus04

My name is **Kumbirai Farai Constance Kupfavira**, a young lady aged 32years. I have a published poetry anthology entitled BANKS by Madhau. Currently I am working with the National Arts Council of Zimbabwe as the Provincial Arts Manager, Midlands Province.

Tafadzwa Chiwanza grew up in Harare. A University of Zimbabwe Accounting student and a poet by calling. His first anthology, *No Bird Is Singing Now*, has been accepted for publication. His work has been featured in various local publications such as The Standard Newspaper's Gourd of consciousness and 3-mob.com.

Edwell Zihonye: The writer has interests in poetry, prose and drama. He is an avid social commentator. He is a teacher at heart and an experienced examiner. He has published poetry, prose and is currently working on a series of Secondary School English Language Textbook series and a play about Cyclone Idai. He has published a novel and three anthologies of poetry. He studied English and History at the University of Zimbabwe.

Troy Da Costa: Once again, this excellent opportunity to contribute to the cultural heritage of Zimbabwe has presented itself and once again, I treated the call for submissions as a call to action. In this collaboration I chose pieces that represent deep personal internal struggles in my preferred Poetic Pros format. I use strong imagery to resonate with everyday issues that most people can identify with. The language used is deliberately free flowing bare basic to encompass all readership levels without feeling patronising or dull. The emotional content of words is where this style should shine bringing understanding and a warm feeling of achievement at the exertion of the reader's imagination.

Wilson Tinotenda Waison is a poet from Chitungwiza, Zimbabwe. A human rights advocate, prose passage writer. Also a brave voice, the Chitungwiza poetry consul of Poets of the World a global platform based on contemporary writings poetasdelmundo.com Waison is the content curator of Deem.lit.org, interviewer of the Contemporary Poetry Online magazine as well as the editor of Whitepages Concept . He is currently doing Journalism at Harare polytechnic.

https://deemliteratureorganisation.wordpress.com

Kabelo is an MSU student from Bulawayo who fell in love with poetry and likes to write poetry because he finds it fun.

Shoko Cosmas Tinashe is a Shona and English poet, writer and upcoming researcher with interest in strategic management and inclusive housing. He was born in 1987 in Zvishavane. He is a Midlands State University Master of Science graduate. His current literary works has been published by Be Zine Magazine (2020), Nango Newsletter (2020). Other previous works were featured in Zimbolicious Volume 1 and Volume 2, Best New African Poets 2017 Anthology, Latin America and Africa Experimental Writing Anthology, Brave Voices Journal 58 2019 (Griots of Oliver Mutukudzi, A special Tribute), Paragon Journal (US), Centum Press (US) and some other poetry magazines and anthologies. Writing is his hobby and life journey.

Mandhla A Mavolwane is a poet and a spoken word artist who writes and performs to entertain, educate and enlighten the masses on the issues affecting our past, present and future. He is currently studying for an undergraduate honours degree in Psychology at the Midlands State University. In terms of his artistry his poems have been published in Best New African Poets 2016, 2017, 2018 & 2019 anthologies, Africa, UK and Ireland: Writing Politics and Knowledge Production Volume 1 and Zimbolicious Volume 3 & 4. Recently he published his first anthology called Ghetto Symphony which can be found on this link http://www.africanbookscollective.com/books/ghetto-symphony

Takunda Shepherd Chikomo is a Zimbabwean author based in Chitungwiza. With three books to his name, "Curtains an anthology of poems", "These things also happened to me" and his latest book "Deflowered", he is one of the most promising writers to emerge out of Zimbabwe and he has just begun!

Johannes Mike Mupisa is a published novelist, academic writer and poet from Mwenezi. He has three books used in the new curriculum that is Gwatakwata Renhetembo -ZJC poetry setbook(Secondary book Publishers(2016); A practical approach to History Studies Book 2(2019) Secondary Book Press and A practical approach to Heritage Studies book 4 (2018). Mupisa resides in Tengera Village in Mwenezi. Johannes Mike

Mupisa got published in several poetry anthologies inclusive of Taura Izwi/Khuluma Izwi/ Speak a Word(2017) comprising of Starbrite finalists. The book was published by Secondary Book Publishers in 2017. Mupisa did not only contribute but also edited the anthology.

Samuel Chuma was born in Gweru, Zimbabwe in 1969. He is married to Semina Hamandishe and the couple are blessed with 3 sons. He lives in Harare, Zimbabwe with his family and works as an Industrial Relations Consultant. Samuel is currently perfecting a collection of poems for publication. The selection featured here is part of that project.

Haile Saize: I born in Harare. Attended Seke 4 Primary and Zengeza 4 High in Chitungwiza. He is currently residing in Cape Town, South Africa. Have been published in Miombo Publishing 2017, Tuck Magazine under The Zimbabwe We Want Campaign 2017, Best New African Poets 2017, Zimbolicious 2018, Echoes of Tumult 2019, Reflection 2020 among other projects.

Chenjerai Mhondera is a poetician, a writest, lord of controversies and a citizen of the world. He is published in over forty publications - anthologies, magazines, blogs, online journals; among lot, including all series of Zimbolicious Poetry, Best New African Poets (BNAP), Chitungwiza Mushamukuru, Mupakwa WeRwendo, Scarlet Anatomy (SA), etc. He has published his own own independent books, including, Mupengo, Masasi aChinoz, A Case of Love and Hate, Ruins of Dambudzo, a series of Hurricane, Manifesto#Anthology, M'cbeth and I, and etc. Chenjerai is also a founder and patron of Writers International Association formerly Writers Club which identifies, nurtures and helps to publish young, up and coming writers in the region and across world.

Oscar Gwiriri is a Certified Forensic Investigations Professional (CFIP) who also holds a *Master of Science Degree in Strategic Management, Bachelor of Business Administration, Associate of Arts in Business Administration Degree, Diploma in Logistics and Transport (CILT, UK)* and a *Diploma in Workplace Safety and Health,* as well as other ten certificates in the fraternity of United Nations Peacekeeping. He was born on 15 June 1975 at Gwiriri Village, Chief Mutasa, Zimbabwe. He attended Manunure

Primary School (Honde Valley) and Dangamvura High School (Mutare). He has more than 25 publications both in English and Shona languages. Oscar is both a creative writer and an academic. He was nominated twice in the National Arts Merits Awards (2019) categories for his books *Hatiponi* and *Chitima nditakure*.

Fudzai Nyarumwe was born in Harare, Zimbabwe in 1999. She attended Glen View 2 Primary School and Watershed College. Fudzai has been enthusiastic about art and design from a very young age. She attended many art camps since she was 6 and won quite a number of accolades due to her competence in drawing and painting. She was a member of the Art Club and Drama Club which awarded her opportunities to take part in the *National Festival of Allied Arts Competitions* in visual arts as well as poetry, and she attained first grades in both aspects. She is a very active person and finds joy in cross country athletics and playing basketball. Fudzai believes that the key to a healthy and fresh mind is through exercising. She reads a lot during her leisure time and enjoys telling stories through writing and painting.

Simbarashe Chirikure was born in 1974 at Musami Hospital, Murehwa District, Zimbabwe. He attended Zengeza 8 Primary School, and Zengeza 2 High School, Chitungwiza. He attained qualifications in Supervisory Management at Management Training Bureau, Masasa, and a Diploma in Business Leadership with the Zimbabwe Institute of Management. Some of his poetry is published in *Hodzeko Yenduri* and *Zimbolicious 3* anthologies.

Natasha Tinotenda Gwiriri was born on 14 May 2000 at Bindura, Zimbabwe. She attended Maneta Primary School (Buhera) and then Mutambara High School (Chimanimani) and Chipadze High School (Bindura). Meanwhile she is doing a Degree in Marketing at Bindura University of Science Education. She is interested in writing poetry and is still experimenting with other literature genres. She is published in *Zimbolicious 3* anthology and *Kwayedza*.

Mildred Mutize, born on 20 April 1983, is a Zimbabwean fiction writer and motivational speaker. Born and raised in Harare, her passion for writing sprouted in her early childhood days and later blossomed during High School where she scooped a number of literature awards. She has authored several short stories which are all hinged on suspense, mystery and thrill. She is married and has three children.

Jabulani Mzinyathi is my name. I am a writer in general and a poet in particular. My poems and other works have been featured in several Zimbabwean and international anthologies. My solo collections are Under The Steel Yoke and Righteous Indignation. I am an avid reader. I enjoy the writing of my compatriot Dambudzo Marechera , Nikolai Gogol, John Steinbeck, Oscar Wilde and many other writers. I am working on several projects namely Covid 19 Diary, Derailed- a novella, Mumambure-a Chishona novel and The African Spirits Speak- which is an arduous identity seeking journey

Zvikomborero Kapuya is a passionate scholar of Afrocentric epistemology and interested in rediscovering Africa. His uses Foacultian, Fanonian, Derridian and Diopian approach in literature, whose mandate is to deconstruct the existing norms of the world co-authored by the imperialism. Currently, he is reading Masters of Science in International Affairs at Midlands State University, he is a holder of Bachelor of Science in Politics and Public Management Honours Degree with First class and Book Prize Award. Zvikomborero Kapuya is from Sanyati rural areas were he did primary education at Javachava Primary School, secondary education at Jompani Secondary School and Advanced Level at Neuso High School

Tinashe Muchuri is a fourth year media student at the Zimbabwe Open University. He is also a poet, storyteller, writer and a freelance journalist. He is the writer of a Shona antinovel, Chibarabada. His poetry appears in the following English Anthologies: *Zimbolicious volume 1, 3 and 4, State of the Nation: Zimbabwe Contemporary Poetry, Daybreak, All Protocols Observed, Visions of Motherland, Defiled Sacredness, War against War, Poems of Solidarity for Haiti, The Writer's Birthday* and in the following magazines: *Parade, Moto, Writer's Scroll, Illuminations 25 and 26, The Warwick Review Vol.III No. 4, Cosumnes River Journal, Rattlesnake Review 22.* His Shona poetry appears in *Jakwara reNhetembo, Mudengu Munei, Dzinonyandura Svinga reNduri, Hodzeko yeNduri, Tipindewo Mudariro* and *Chitubu.* Both his English and Shona poetry appear in online journals, magazines, blogs and websites. He enjoys imbibing the Indigenous Knowledge and is a blogger who blogs in Shona at *http//:mudararatinashemuchuri.blogspot.com* and a Contributing Editor Shona section at Munyori Online Literal Journal and a columnist with *WinZimbabweblogspot*. He is working towards his second Shona novel to be launched in October 2020 titled, Zvavanhu Herevo!

Zimbabwean born, South African based artist **Kudakwashe K Nhevera** is a passionate and versatile artist who specialises in pencil sketches and oil paintings. Most of his work revolves around portraiture and modes of transport derived from his fascination with movement. He has explored other mediums and subjects before settling for these and constantly strives to improve himself and his work.

Introduction

Zimbolicious Anthology: An Anthology of Zimbabwean Literature and Arts, Vol 5 is the fifth in this yearly journal of Zimbabwean literature and the arts as it happens. We started this anthology in 2016 and we are going strong yearly. This year's anthology is strong in poetry especially Shona poetry which has remained vibrant and a staple to this anthology. The poetry covers a range of subjects; love, spirituality, religion, migration, poet's vocation and as usual the political direction or situation in the country

The fiction deals with a wide range issues, from religious contrivance in Gwiriri's story, drug problem and corruption in Mutize's story, the political and economic strife in Tokwe's story, and the personal trauma story in Chikomo's car accident story. Each story is jagged, painful and beautifully crafted.

In the nonfiction section we have Muchuri's illuminating essay on another Zimbabwe storyteller, Ignitious Mabasa's Shona books, Zvikomborero Kapuya harks back to the land issue as the starting point and catapult to the misunderstandings between Zimbabwe and her erstwhile foreign enemies, Chikono writes his painful life story on shame families carry when a family member has a child out of wedlock, worst when the child is disabled and Mwanaka has a small philosophical vignette essay on choice.

The visual section is heralded by Nhevera's iconic brushworks depicting movement and portraiture, and Mwanaka has an array of art pieces from documentary photography, experimental photography, water colour, computer graphic and installation, wrapping up this new offering.

Our job is to discover new writing and art talent in the country which we didn't disappoint this year by unfurling 10 new writers who haven't previously been published here or elsewhere and keeping a bunch of those we have been publishing over the past 5 years, thus we are continuing developing Zimbabwe writing, literature and arts in our own way, and we hope to create a large body of Zimbabwe authorship, writings and art.

Nonfiction

From Colonial Master to Enemy: Issues Behind Zimbabwe-Britain Relations in Post-Humanistic Histories.

Zvikomborero Kapuya

Abstract

The study examines the British-Zimbabwe relations in the 21st century and adopts a rigorous intellectual analysis of some of the unchartered terrains of knowledge. It is argued that, coloniality of land, power and global space is the main driver of the hostility since Zimbabwe's protracted land struggle from 1893-2002 threatened Pax Britannica and Western hegemony, resulted to sanctions. In current media reportage and literature, it is argued that, Zimbabwe was sanctioned as a result of non-compliance to the dictates of democracy and property rights through orchestrated violent land invasion without compensations, but history repeats itself, what happened in 1893-1896 also happened in 21st century were land was given back to the original owners. The research use desktop reviews and employ Transmodenity, post-structural, realism and post-modern theories to cement arguments.

Key Words: Land, Coloniality, Decoloniality, Zimbabwe, Britain

Introduction

International system is characterized by the discourse of change and continuity, that parade as the dynamics of international relations. The central issue of this article is the factors that led to the deterioration of the relations between Zimbabwe and the West, there are number of factors that establish an epistemic hypothesis over this phenomenon. The relations between Zimbabwe and the West date back in pre-colonial, colonial and post-colonial episodes, in this question the main focus is 'post-colonial Zimbabwe". To comprehend this discourse, the philosophical thoughts of Zimbabwe-West relations informed by theories of the international relations that simply explain the behaviors of the state in global affairs. Fukuyama (1991) coin the theory of 'end of history' whereby the liberal-capitalist triumph over socialism, but 21st century political affairs proves Francis Fukuyama theory wrong, the centrality of the discourse of relations and conflicts in Zimbabwe-West relations remain a key evidence to object the claim of 'end of history'. It can be said, 'history truly was ended but returned from vacation in the post-millennium society'. There are various factors that deteriorate relations of Zimbabwe-West, manifest in form of political, social and economic, however basing on this means of analysis, termed the trinity of analysis by Wallenstein (1991), argues that it limits the analytical concept of the discourse hence this article is focusing much on developing the epistemology of foreign policy analytics and the issues that led to the sour relations of Zimbabwe and the West. Political factors are more important in this discourse, since politics define the global interaction, issues of anti-imperial legacy, land redistribution, democratic crisis and abuse of human rights (property rights), however there are some other factors to look on for instance, social factors such as racism and economic factors as to proffer a clear proposition of the central problem. Events such as land reform programme, sanctioning of Zimbabwe, electoral violence and the Look East Policy are key concepts in elucidating the factors that contributed to the deterioration of Zimbabwe-West relations. To engage in critical taxonomy of this aspect, realism theory, game theory, idealism theory, dependency theory and Marxist theories provides a theoretical paradigm to comprehend the contemporaneous issues of Zimbabwe international relations.

Intellectual Analysis of the Issues Behind: Confrontation or Justice?

To commence, the issue of land reform policy remains a central issue in the understanding of the deterioration of Zimbabwe-West relations. The available literature engages in researches from different disciplines with different narratives that are informed by Chimurenga culture and non-partisan perspectives (Mahomva 2016). The idea of decolonization was an unfinished project in 1980, whereby means of production controlled by few white minorities protected by colonial Westminster legal statutes,

3

the Lancaster House Constitution, Chapter two on Human rights. Against this background, land was the central issues of conflict during the war of liberation struggle (Muchemwa 2013, Mutizira 2008 and Nyawo 2012). This simply explains that, land was the strategic factor for Zimbabwe diplomatic relations with the West, hence Mugabe regime embarked on land reform programme as to achieve the objectives of War of Liberation Struggle and decolonization.

"For a colonized people the most essential value, because it is the most concrete, is first and foremost the land: the land which will bring them bread and, above all, dignity" (Frantz Fanon 1963).

In Fanonian school of thought, the marginalization of blacks (dames) to reserves matured into conflict, that kick started the project of liberation, later continued in the post-colonial Zimbabwe. As to establish a post-colonial society, Mugabe's regime embarked on Land Reform policy, sloganized the motto of correcting imbalances and termed it "Hondo yeminda" (war of land). This event created a most decisive effect to the almost tattered Zimbabwe-West relations, and violated the Lancaster House Conference Agreement of the land question and white settler. In analysis, the Fanonian school of thought provides an epistemic paradigm about the value of land, whereby it gives dignity to the people and above all as source of economic production, against this aspect the political reclamation of land by the native Zimbabweans who were once marginalized in the colonial era, aimed to restore the dignity and pride, affected Zimbabwe's foreign affairs. The land question contributed immensely to the deterioration of Zimbabwe-West relations.

Furthermore, the aspect of anti-neocolonial campaign manifest in the philosophy of Mugabeism had much effect in further tearing apart the relationship between Zimbabwe and the West. Scholars and diplomats, largely concern about the logic behind the deterioration of Zimbabwe-West relations in the post-colonial Africa, the main causative agent is the issue of realization of the continuity of global coloniality and offer an anti-imperial solution to the problem. Mugabeism defined by Ndhlovu-

4

Gatsheni (2006 and 2009) as a philosophy that shapes Mugabe views of the declaration of the anti-imperial wars. The projected relations between Zimbabwe-West adequately described by Walter Rodney (1974) as the main reason that unfolds the story of underdevelopment, whereby colonialism and neo-colonialism deprived the development of the developing countries. North-South Relations (Gunder Frank 1993, Samir Amin 2009, Mignolo, 2013) characterized by the exploitation of the periphery by the core whereby capitalist countries developed their economies at the expense of developing countries. Quinjano (2000) coined it as global coloniality, whereby North-South relations structured in the economic zones, the dichotomy of developed and developed. The realization of the 'post-colonial neocolonized state' (Spivak 2010, Mbembe 2000 and Ndlovu-Gatsheni 2013) created hostilities between Zimbabwe and West, the Western countries wanted to continue to dominate in global affairs through control of world economies envisaged by capitalist-liberal ideology, however Zimbabwe under Mugabe regime crafted policies such as indigenization and land reform to dismantle the global-capitalist tendencies.

> "I am still the Hitler of the time, This Hitler has only one objective, justice for his own people, sovereignty for his people, recognition of the independence of his people, and their rights to their resources. If that is Hitler, then let me be Hitler tenfold, ten times that what we stand for" (Mugabe 2003)

From Mugabeism perspective, his policies threatened the outside world and influenced the dynamics of Zimbabwe foreign relations, the issue of preserving sovereignty was the mandatory prognosis of Mugabe regime, realizing the dangers of neocolonialism and put measures. In analysis, the relationship between Zimbabwe and the west deteriorated for political rise that was informed by the conflict of hegemonic interest and anti-imperial interest, clashes to conceive the hostility between the West and Zimbabwe.

More so, the deterioration of Zimbabwe-West relations influenced the dynamics of international politics in the 21st century. The main reason was the political contestation of ideologies, whereby Zimbabwe engaged in the movement of calling for reforming the most controversial global governance headed by the United Nations Security Council (UNSC). This has been posing an extraordinary threat to the United States hegemony, since the multipolarity and balance of power concert in the 21st century is shrouded in mystery (Mearsheimer 2001) and the United States engaged in offensive campaign of creating the unipolar society through influencing the structures of social and political values. Robert Gabriel Mugabe once denounced the global injustices, the inversion of Iraq by United States of America (2001), invasion of Libya by North Atlantic Treaty Organization (NATO), the Cambodia question, operationalization of CIA in Africa and various injustices by the West. According to Blair and Curtis (2009) and Chomsky (2016) United States of America inversion of Iraq was inspired by the national interest rather than the issues of Weapons of Mass Destruction (WMD) and democratization project. Against this issue, it raised hostility since Robert Mugabe denounced the evils of the West publicly in United Nations Summit and various gathering. In 2004, George W Bush stated that the policies of Robert Mugabe posed an extraordinary threat to United States foreign policy, and a decade later Barak Obama repeated the same statement and tightened sanction measures on Zimbabwe. In this regard, the United States project is a history of glory and aligning herself with moral-humanistic values and sloganize democratic-capitalist ideology as global political values, hence Zimbabwe actions towards exposing the nonrealistic politics of the West deteriorated the relations. In this regard, Zimbabwe emerged as the voice of the voiceless, that champion the global reformist paradigm in the international system, hence it attracted few friends from the East and parade of enemies from the West, therefore this is the central reason in understanding Zimbabwe-West hostilities.

The deterioration of Zimbabwe-West relations in post-colonial politics informed by democratic conundrum in the coffers of Zimbabwe body politic, Sachikonye (2011) states that, Zimbabwe embarked on land reform programme as an economic redemptive programme, however at the same time democratic principle was violated, the notion of property rights. The violent occupation of white farms in the year 2002 without compensation violated Britain and Zimbabwe diplomatic agreements at Lancaster house Conference and All Donors Conference in the 1990s. The case of Von Abbo, De Freeth v Republic of Zimbabwe prosecuted by SADC Tribunal rule in favor of white farmers, however due to nature of the international law, whereby it was voluntary and not enforceable (Dugard 2009) the Zimbabwean government refused to implement the judgement and continued land distribution without compensation. This issue led to the sanctioning of Zimbabwe by the European Union through Cotonou Partnership Agreement Article 96 and United States ZIDERA of 2002 (Zimbabwe Democratic Economic Recovery Act), this signalled the deterioration of Zimbabwe-West relations in the 21st century. The Zimbabwean government was accused of being undemocratic by the West, therefore the issue of sanctions were justified. In an attempt to re-engage with the West, Emmerson Mnangagwa administration failed to impress the West due to alledged electoral rigging, 1 August 2018 army killing the civilians and the Internet shutdown and continued killings in January that led to sanctioning again of Zimbabwe. In this regard, the triumph of liberal ideology after the collapse of Union Soviet Socialist Republic (USSR) created the new world order that valued democracy as the best form of government and informed by democratic peace theory proposed by Immanuel Kant in 18th Century, hence Western capitalist engaged in foreign policy campaign of democratizing the world that is evidenced by the collapse of dictatorship in Middle East, Asia, Latin America and Africa (Mearsheimer 2001). In analysis, the failure of the democratic project due to controversial land reforms and alleged political violence from the year 2000 to present deteriorated the relations between the West and Zimbabwe, and led to the sanctions and coercive measure for political reformation in Zimbabwe.

However, social factors also contributed immensely to the disintegration of the relations between Zimbabwe and the West in the 21st Century, manifest in racial lines of sociological schema. For Asante (1991, 2003, 2007) and Mazama (2003), the problem with post-colonial state is it treated the effects of colonialism as only political and economic forgetting the mental effects to the colonized society. Mkandawire (2012) penned an article titled "generation of African scholars" whereby first generation of African scholars' over-exhaust the economic effects of colonialism in a Marxist perspective and failed to understand its mental effects. Ngugi wa Thiongo (1983) proposed the theory of decolonizing the mind, but based it on language and culture, whereby the relegation of native languages to the bottom in public communication created the other and alienated Africans from Africa. This particular conception is a major conceptual issue in understanding the contemporary Zimbabwe-West relations.

> "One of the most powerful myths of the twentieth century was the notion that the elimination of colonial administrations amounted to the myth of a 'post-colonial world. The heterogeneous and multiple global structures put in place over a period of 450 years did not evaporate with juridical political decolonization of the periphery over the past 50 years. We continue to live under the same 'colonial power matrix' with juridical-political decolonization we moved from a period of 'global colonialism' to the current period of global coloniality" (Grosfoguel 2007;219).

Ramon Grosfoguel coined the theory of global coloniality, that simply explains the continuity of colonialism, whereby coloniality of being manifests in racial form. The global society lacked the system of heterachies (Kontopolous) but employed hierarchy due to racism. In colonial times, native Africans where ghettoized by the colonialist, that even continue in the post-colonial society and still cherish the idea of inequality. In this regard, the Zimbabwean government embarked on land reform programme as to restore racial power to the black society and dismantle the coloniality of being, whereby the society was structured in dichotomies of rational-irrational, inferior-superior, primitive-civilized and traditional-modern (Quinjano 2000), ghetto and suburbs. In analysis, the relationship between Zimbabwe and the West due to colonialism and post-colonial coloniality exploded into hatred, whereby the social calling for correcting racial imbalances penned the hatred between Zimbabwe and the West.

Conclusion: Mapping the contours of the Future

In conclusion, Zimbabwe-West relations remain the most important issue in the study of global diplomacy and foreign policy. The dynamics of this relations influences the structural shift of global politics and power relations. The relationship between Zimbabwe-West has triple heritage from pre-colonial, colonial and post-colonial, but the central problem was the question of the genuineness of the relations. Realist philosophers, put forward the idea of state interaction in the international system is defined by state interest (survival) and struggle for power. In contrary to realist school of thoughts, idealists believe that post-1945 global society is informed by the ideal of quest for peace and co-operation for peace and developmental purposes. Bridging the gap between these two dominating paradigms of the international relations, dependency theory emerges from the Carribean-Hispanophone society and the global society, defined Africa's underdevelopment as rooted in North-South relations and exploitation by the developed countries. These theories provide a distinctive scholarship paradigm of the central problem of Zimbabwe-West relations that even continue to deteriorate in post-Mugabe era. The main problematic issues discussed in this essay, but mainly 'high politics', play a central role to comprehend the discourses. The issues of land reform, democratic crisis, political call for reforming global politics and imperial blockade has a major effect in deteriorating the relations between Zimbabwe and the West in the 21st Century. The politics of the 21st century, informed by 9/11 attack and the controversial issues of Zimbabwe, however social factors such as dismantling racism fabricated as a result of slavery (William, 2002), colonialism and coloniality created a compositive feature that later exploded as land reform and indigenization policies as the project of decolonization. The new world order politics is not about the end of history or the triumph of liberal-capitalist, it's about issues of creating heterachies, recognizing the small state's sovereignty and their impact in global affairs and the rise of China, creating the hopes of the existence of global multi-polar system.

References

Amin, S. (1990) Delinking, Zed Books

Asante, M.K. (1991) 'The Afrocentricity Idea in Education", Journal of Negro Education

Asante, M.K. (2003) Afrocentricity; The Theory of Social Change, Illinois; African American Images

Asante, M.K. (2007) An Afrocentric Manifesto; Cambridge; Polity Press

Fanon, F. (1963) The Wretched of the Earth, Paris; Penguin

Grosfoguel, R. (2007) The Epistemic Decolonial Turn; Towards Global Political Economy; Duke University Press.

Gunder Frank, A. (1984) Critique and Anti-Critique; Essays on Dependency and Reformism, London; Macmillan

Mahomva, R.R. (2016) Chimurenga Culture in Contemporary Society, Bulawayo; Leaders of Africa Network;

Mandani, M. (1998) Citizen and the Subject; Contemporary Africa and the Legacy of Late Colonialism; Kampala; Makerere University

Mazama, A. ed(2003) The Afrocentric Paradigm, Trenton; Africa World Press

Mazrui, A. (2002) Africanity Redefined, Chicago; Chicago university Press

Mignolo, W.D. (2011) The darker Side of Western Modernity; Global Futures, Decolonial Options, Durham; Duke University Press.

Mkandawire, T. (2013) Three Generations of African Scholars

Muchemwa, T. (2012) Struggle for Land in Zimbabwe from 1966-2010, Harare; Heritage Publishers

Mtizira, N. (2008) The Chimurenga Protocol, Harare; Weaver Press

Ndlovu-Gatsheni, S.J. (2000) Do Zimbabwe Exist? Trajectories of Nationalism, National Identity Formation and Crisis in Post-Colonial State, Peter Lang

Ndlovu-Gatsheni, S.J. (2013) Coloniality of Power in Post-Colonial Africa; Myths of Decolonization, Dakar; CODESERIA

Ndlovu-Gatsheni, S.J. (2015) Mugabeism? History, Politics and Power in Zimbabwe, London; Palgrave Macmillan

Ngugi wa Thiongo. (1981) decolonizing the Mind, Politics of Language in Africa, New York; Heinemann

Nyawo, V.Z. (2012) Dilemmas of Agrarian Reform in Independent Zimbabwe and South Africa, Gweru; Mambo Press

William, C. (1992) Destruction of Black Civilization; Chicago; Chicago University Press.

Quinjano, A. (2000) Coloniality of Power and Eurocentrism in Latin America, International Sociology, volume 15 (2) pp215-232

Sachikonye, L. (2011) When a State Turns of Its Citizens. Institutionalized Violence and Political Culture, Harare; Weaver Press

Spivak, G. C. (1994) Can Subaltern Speak, Delhi; Stefan Nowotny Publishers

Innovative Storytelling and the Future of Shona Folktales in Zimbabwe: A Study of Ignatius Mabasa's tales.

Tinashe Muchuri
Zimbabwe Open University

ABSTRACT

*I*ndigenous Knowledge Systems comprise of the bodies of knowledge created by the ancestors in Africa as footprints through which the present and future generations are able to see the future. Storytelling has been lagging behind though it is a major part of the Shona society's moral, ethical, knowledge builder, and entertainment. Of late an upsurge of storytellers moving away from telling stories around fires during the night is increasing. Due to the change of times storytellers are following children wherever they are. Some scholars underplay the role being played by Ignatius Mabasa in developing storytelling and in mapping the Shona folklore future in Zimbabwe. This chapter critically examined Mabasa's innovative storytelling approach in the 21st century as a performer and contemporary' Shona folklore writer. Furthermore, the chapter investigated whether new storytelling techniques are making the Shona folklore relevant, competing with new technological advancement; interrogated the forms that Mabasa's tales are created in, challenges encountered in the creation process and in marketing concept and how the creator overcomes the impedance. Moreso the chapter looked at sustainability of Mabasa's innovative ideas and the milestones made or opportunities that can be exploited in sustaining storytelling in Zimbabwe and Africa at large. Employing Critical Discourse Analysis theory the paper utilized a descriptive content analysis approach of Mabasa's two tales to identify innovative traits that promote Shona storytelling sustainability. While appreciating Mabasa's creativity and dedication to innovative storytelling the paper interrogated the supposition behind the portrayal of Baboon and Hare characters in modern costumes and utilizing modern props viewed by cultural conservationists as harmful to indigenous cultural practices. It therefore attempted to deeper questions about the posterity of indigenous knowledge systems in order to promote innovation and sustainability of storytelling in Shona relevant to the contemporary society.

Key words: Innovation, Indigenous Knowledge Systems, Sustainable Storytelling.

INTRODUCTION

According to World Book Dictionary (1992) refer innovation as 'a change made in the established way of doing things' and Oxford Advanced Learner's Dictionary (2010) defines innovation as 'the introduction of new things, ideas, or ways of doing things.' I also add that innovation is a disruptive force that changes, improves, or distorts the status quo or reshape old ideas in order to make them adapt to new spaces, time, and location, technology and that to be innovative is to be adventurous, to be brave, to be committed, to be confident, to be dedicated, to be determined to face challenges with a new thought or a revamped thought regardless of risks envisioned or discouragements along the way in order to achieve a goal of easy of doing things.

Indigenous is a belonging to a particular place rather than coming from somewhere (Oxford Advanced Learner's Dictionary, 2010) else hence indigenous knowledge systems are bodies of knowledge created by the ancestors as footprints through which the present and future generations are able to pass insights, wisdom, ideas and perceptions and the history from one generation to the next generation.

Storytelling is a way of recording and expressing one's feelings and attitudes as responses to what one experienced around one's environment (Gbadegesin, 1984) and retelling it to a single listener or more through voice and gestures (Ngugi, 1986).

Learning Shona enhances imagination and strengthens critical understanding of issues (Mufanechiya and Mufanechiya, 2015:43) and Grant (1989) avers that children taught culture in their languages appreciate stories of own country more and probably contribute to the stories when grown up, constructing a rational and reasonable person in their relationship with nature and other human beings.

African storytelling is attributed to construct, uphold good social order and as a way of passing on traditions, codes and values (Vambe. 2001) explaining natural phenomena, teaching morality, provide African people with a sense of identity, entertainment of the community (Ngugi wa Thiong'o 1982). Storytelling enhances thinking, expand knowledge, community building and develop public speaking skills (Mabasa, 2014).

This essay highlights milestones achieved by Mabasa's storytelling innovation and opportunities laid bare in print, audio, online or visual motivating listeners to be willing participants and creators.

Storytelling is a proven solid early childhood development tool that premised on in the past and has become critical during Zimbabwe's updated curriculum overhaul based on the Nziramasanga commission report (1999).

In the past storytelling by parents, grandparents, aunts, uncles and children learning to become part of the storytelling community was a common learning institute. Modern education systems shifted Shona storytelling as it borrows from other knowledge systems in what the Shona say, 'ideas are like fire, they are borrowed (Mazano moto anogokwa) laying bare that Shona knowledge systems were ever in motion in recording of history, bringing and inspiring new ideas attesting to what Obioha (2015) and Vambe (2001) posit that, "No culture can claim absolute sufficiency. There is something every culture lacks but which it needs" and that Storytelling is a rich repository of norms, morals and values, celebration, warning, mourning or entertainment.

Mabasa (2019) adds that Storytellers create stories not from the blue but are usually influenced by their society answering to the assertion that says, best writers are those who write about their environment. In the Shona context Mabasa has made great strides towards innovation and sustainability of storytelling through adapting new technologies and the changing firesides.

Zimunya (2018)'s assertion that 'if you marginalize a language, you marginalize a people' as a response to the proclamation and recognisation of 16 local languages in the Constitution of Zimbabwe (Act No.20) 2013 without putting mechanism through which these languages would be used and learned. The embracing of storytelling by the updated primary and secondary education curriculum, United Nations (UN) promulgation of 2019 as a year of indigenous languages, the outcry by 2013 ZIBF Writers Workshop attendees denouncing Mabasa's Redhiyo yaTsuro as a rebellious attempt by a language dissident to destroy Shona knowledge systems as a reflection of the changing firesides informs the need for this chapter.

United Nations General Assembly dedicated the year 2019 as The International Year of Indigenous Languages focusing at the marginalized languages of the people from Polar Circles, Arabian Peninsula, Australia, East Asia and Central America and was celebrated as a way of raising awareness of critical risks these languages face and their value as medium of culture, knowledge systems and ways of life. UN has seen that indigenous languages are an investment in spearheading their communities' destinies as well as participating in their country's economic, cultural, and political life; providing 'unique systems and understanding of the world, sustainable development, peace building and reconciliation, fundamental human rights and freedoms for indigenous peoples, social inclusiveness, literacy, poverty reduction and international cooperation, cultural values, diversity and heritage.'

This chapter concurs with the adage that, change is not easy to embrace as Mabasa's innovative Shona storytelling encountered a stiff societal repudiations and brickbats as conservationists argue that they cannot allow their Baboon and Hare stories to be mutilated and decimated by contemporaries instead the contemporaries should use other characters for their stories not their beloved Gudo naTsuro. Mabasa (2013) at the ZIBF Writers Workshop held at the National Gallery of Zimbabwe was labelled cultural sinner who needs deliverance, a rebel and irresponsible cultural dissident masquerading as a writer and storyteller and a mischief taking folktales to new technologies and give characters modern props (Mabasa 2014). Wasamba weighs him down arguing that taking folklore to new technologies is a mischief and making Tsuro slove modern things defile folktales.

Mabasa(2014) further contends that, "Folktales should be made exciting and relevant so that our children today do not lose interest in that heritage just because it is not responding to social change

In addition Mabasa (2014) argues that learners are moulded around being pragmatic against theoretic hence the call for innovative ideas to secure storytelling sustainability. However, this has created the impression that the new storytellers are mutating indigenous knowledge systems for the benefiting imperialistic views. Conservationist demanded that every storyteller involving Tsuro naGudo should follow the structure, the settings and use props that were used in the ancient storytelling sessions implying that Hare and Baboon stories should not move with times. Yet Shona ancestors assert that, **'Kare haagari ari kare' and 'Gore harizi pakaza rimwe' or 'Chinokura chinokotama musoro wegudo chava chinokoro'** an admission that life changes, everything changes and therefore change must be embraced relevantly and storytellers should thus follow the changing firesides in order to sustain Shona storytelling and be able to solve current poblems.

Mushava (2016, 2019) describes Mabasa as a 'disruptive innovator of the Shona novel'. Mabasa is indeed a disciple of the Shona wisdom which embraces change. Muyambo (2016) attests that Mabasa followed the dictates of the Shona tradition of embracing change and move with times. However this chapter discovers that Mabasa is among other innovators who maybe by fate fell on the wayside after being attacked by the Shona language conservationists. There is a time when Tsuro and Gudo were recorded jumping fences to steal milk at a farm and also stole sacks of orange. There is also a time when Tsuro was recorded as farmers together with Gudo and animals like Nzou and Mhembwe. Hassan Musa together with the Literature Bureau tried to bring the story into the city with the publication of Hassan Musa comic books. Mbuya Tendai Makura weighed in with her Zimbabwe Children's Literature Foundation which published quite a number of folktales which were a rendition of

16

tales children grew up hearing from their parents and grandparents but were coming in hard copies and some accompanied with audio cassettes. The Zimbabwe Children's Literature Foundation published Gombiro (1985) Tsuro in 'Tsuro Kanoshereketa' where Tsuro went on a journey meeting people digging for mice without a hoe that he lent his hoe **'Ndinoda mukaka wangu. Kana musina motondiripa nebadza iro'** and he was given the hoe. He also met people constructing a road and eating sadza with mufushwa and offered them his mice on condition they eat the mice and serve him with soup. They could not honour their promise. They compensated him with a gun which he later gave to a king who wanted to scare away pigs which were destroying his fields. The king broke the gun and compensated him with a beautiful girl Runako and speaks of her as someone whom he cannot give to anyone because he wants her to brew him tea rich in milk. ***"Kuseka zvangu mukoma wangu uyu mukadzi wangu, ndinoda kuti anobika tii hobvu kumba kwangu'.*** Throughout this tale only props have changed but everything else remained the same in what Mabasa (2014) argues,

Tsuro's wit and tricks should not be confined to the old ... our Tsuro just like our changing lifestyles should also adapt or else he will die because he will lose relevance. It is not only Tsuro's setting that needs an overhaul, but his language also, yet returning those hunhu/ubuntu values we hold dear and that hold us together as a people (Mabasa, 2014).

Thereby concurring with Gbadegesin (1984) who says storytelling is a recording and expressing of one's feelings and attitudes as responses to what one experienced around one's environment. It is unfortunate that though Gombiro is one of the innovators of the Shona Folktales he suffered the writer of one story syndrome.

Tsuro naGudo story stayed in confines of the farms, bush and the rural areas until Mabasa emerged with innovative ideas of telling it using modern props, settings like the urban areas and depicting the lives of modern people living in the urban areas and giving Baboon and Hare the power to acquire modern utility products as those used in today's civilized world and also utilizing many available mediums through which these tales can be accessed by the audience.

17

KUWANDA HUUYA KWAKARAMBWA NEMUROYI

Shona knowledge systems accept and appreciate migrants into its territories. There are stories and monuments constructed by the Shona people but with time many things happened and names of certain places changed to new historical names. In ancient Shona society there were places like Manyanga, Matonjeni, Dzimbabwe and Dungwiza now by these new names Ntabazinduna, Matopos, Great Zimbabwe and Chitungwiza respectively? Why then should the story remain stagnant without being relevant to this day when proverbs show that Shona knowledge systems embrace diversity. In Redhiyo yaTsuro, Shumba tells Tsuro to return the gadget where he had found it. Shumba's and Nzou's act can be referred to as the act of conservationists denying innovation in storytelling.

RUZIVO MOTO UNOGOKWA

Shona knowledge systems encourage borrowing of ideas and are very clear on what should be borrowed and how it should be borrowed. Ideas should be borrowed, but should be tested, measured according to Shona knowledge before using then. Hence **zano pangwa une rakowo**. Since the Shona borrows, there is agreement that knowledge is not stagnant but flows like spring water which continues bringing out fresh and refreshing water. Shumba and other animals in Redhiyo yaTsuro interrogated Tsuro's watch idea that he brought into the jungle. They found it useless and not relevant in the bush hence returning it to the storekeeper for swap and top. A modern day business concept in the informal computer and mobile phone business In Redhiyo yaTsuro, Tsuro tells Kamba that a radio transmit local and international news (**inotaura nyaya dzemuno nedzekunze**) and that was the reason why he had brought the radio into their territory so that he could be aware of what is happening in the other worlds. Tsuro alludes to globalisation. He wanted to be a global citizen. Furthermore the Shona says, **Kugara nhaka huona dzevamwe** -We copy from others for us to use our heritage well. Stagnant water is a source of dangerous water borne diseases such as malaria, diarrhoea, typhoid, cholera hence ideas that remain idle and constant is a breeding space for failure. Flowing water is safe except it is polluted from the source or from its tributaries hence Shona people should be aware of what they accept therefore **zano pangwa une rako** (receive advice benchmarking with your own).

For foreigners and their ideas to say, they should be agreeing with Shona values are good and if not they are thrown away. Ideas only co-habit if they agree. It is hard to live together without mutual understanding, hence in Redhiyo yaTsuro, when all the animals refused to let Tsuro stay with the watch, he went back to the storekeeper to do as swap and top for a radio. When Tsuro failed to make peace with others in the jungle he did the only noble thing according to Shona knowledge system, to make peace with others by asking for forgiveness. **Kugara kunzwana**, Tsuro says, "I am sorry my friends, I wanted to get news about other places and also to get entertained by the music **(Ndiregereiwo shamwari dzangu, ndanga ndichidawo kuziva zvinhu zvinoitika kune dzimwe nzvimbo pamwe chete nekunakidzwa nemagitare.)**

KUKANYA HURANGANA

Mabasa mainly tell stories in Shona and sometimes code switches to English as matter of accommodating non-Shona speaking audience complies with the proverb **kugara hunzwana**, that encourages people to live together and only if they understand one another. Ngugi wa Thiongo in *Decolonising the mind* (1987) alludes to the importance of using one's language when expressing important ideas that impact the African community. In Redhiyo yaTsuro, Tsuro buys a watch that he uses to measure time needed to do each activity. Tsuro took his watch around, showing off to relatives. Other animals refused to entertain Tsuro's watch, his idea was not accommodated. It had no takers. In a Shona village, you have to consult first before implementation. Tsuro brought new ideas because he was the most travelled person in their society but those who stayed behind did not blindly accept his borrowed ideas without censoring it. The society has a way of taking in innovative ideas that are good and healthy for its development. This exposes the democratic side of the Shona society because for every decision is after consultation and interrogation. Once the idea is found to be good it sails through making the Shona being socially inclusive. In Redhiyo yaTsuro, Tsuro acted without consulting the other citizens of the jungle hence he found himself isolated. 'Tsuro was troubled a lot. He sat on top of a rock and switched off the radio (**Tsuro kanetseka kwazvo. Akagara Padombo, achibva adzima redhiyo yake).**' He did self evaluation decided how to mend his ways with everyone, He decided to consult Kamba whom he persuaded to intermediate between him and the rest of the jungle citizens. When Kamba asked him what is the thing that was making the noise, Tsuro answers that, "It is technology Kamba … Technology is moving with times (**Inonzi tekinoroji Kamba! … Tekinoroji ndiko kufambirana nenguva**)." Mabasa expresses that, a people who doesn't accept change and innovation dies, concurring with Shona saying that says **gore harizi pakaza rimwe** (Years are not the same, they change).

However as innovative ideas stir our thinking; people should remember Shona wise counsel that **Mvura bvongodzi ndiyo garani**. Innovative ideas unsettles the status quo, it changes the way things were being done, it unravels some furs, but eventually everything settles down and the community celebrates with the innovator and true to Mabasa's words that:

> *Our problem is in wasting time in lamenting that we are not given space to express ourselves, on the internet, or on many platforms in the world, and if you ask them what they are doing they tell you things are hard and I as a person in the field of writing has taken upon myself to write the tales, to help preserve them. (Mabasa. 2014)*

Fortune (1982) asserts that storytelling by parents is more concerned with planting and maintaining discipline and attitudes in their children and that by grandparents' aims at correcting misdeeds. In Kunene (1991), he concurs that lessons derived from African stories teach children about moralities by giving them a sense of belonging and indentify. In Chipo neChipopai, Chipo meets Chipopai eating the pie. For parents to correct their children it means they should be continuously monitoring their children's daily activities making the issues contemporary, therefore there is need for storytellers to strive to be relevant to their current situation by telling appropriate stories hence Mabasa argues that he is not reinventing the wheel because even in the past there is a Shona tale of Gudo naTsuro tales used technologies of their contemporary times. It concurs with Ngugi (1982) assertion that borrows props and developments in keeping the people's history alive.

Today, Mabasa is his audiences' darling; was engaged by the First Lady Amai Auxilia Mnangagwa to be part of Amai neNgano, Star Fm for Ngano programme, and NGOs to write tales that help create awareness on different phenomena.

IMBWA INOROVERWA PACHINYIRO

Chipo neChipopai is a short tale yet packed with meaning. It is among what Fortune categorised as tales told by parents to instil corrective behaviour in their children. Though it is in Shona, Chipo neChipopai is dealing with global topical themes of early child marriages and children sexual abuse. Mabasa places the community in a Kombi that included activists who know about child rights and who understand the power of citizen's arrest that can be effected on child abusers and other offenders before handing them over to police law to take its course. The activists in the kombi did not wait long to arrest Chipopai because Shona knowledge systems advise that time does not wait for anyone (**Nguva haimirire munhu)** and also that a dog must be punished at the crime scene (**imbwa inoroverwa pachinyiro)**. Chipopai tried to run away but was caught and brought before the court of law where he was sentenced to spent a long time in the prison. Here, Mabasa brings children to the things they are familiar with and things they love to have but used as baits used by their abusers. Children know that ice cream is bought in supermarkets and thus Chipo and Chipopai go to the supermarket to buy the ice cream. These are children's lived experiences and environments

21

that will lure them to the story as the storyteller narrates the events. Mabasa is therefore not running away from the dictates of knowledge systems but evolves within the confines of Shona knowledge systems innovatively by modernizing the tale bringing in new technology for easy accessibility by modern audiences on WhatsApp, Youtube, Facebook and Google search. He is simply following the changing firesides which are now found on television, radio, online, and mobile phones. The act by Zimbabwe's Ministry of Primary and Secondary Education to approve tales use in schools is a refreshing and innovative milestone that brings the people together to discuss topical issues in a short time. The commuters therefore contest the assertions that say 'there is no hurry in Africa' and that 'Africans lack urgency'.

REGAI DZIVE SHIRI MAZAI HAANA MUTO

Chipo neChipopai fits well with the proverb, 'let them be birds, eggs have no soup; (regai dzive shiri mazai haana muto). There is no record of people being imprisoned or punished for abusing children to the level it has been now. Mabasa moved with times as Chipo naChipopai criminalizes early marriage as opposed to the past's moral grounding where instead of criminalizing the abuser, the parents would demand payment of lobola. Mabasa shows that change can be achieved without moving away from self but just reorient one's past in order to fit in the demands of the modern fast society. Short tales find its way easy on radio and television programmes as fillers. After unsettling the longer narratives, Mabasa's short versions like the Tshaka's assegai has find its takers as the Ministry of Primary and Secondary education has approved some of his tales to be used in the curriculum. On 25 May 2019 Mabasa was telling the African diplomatic community stories as they commemorated Africa Day. Mabasa (2019) posits that storytelling helps people to understand different society's myriad phenomena and challenges and how such can be solved;

Perhaps children are seeing action films with fighting people where they are killing each other with guns which doesn't help. We grew up knowing that, a young one of a leopard is the one which grew up fighting. In Tales, fights are there but they are solved amicably allowing the society to move on and also helping children to learn how to solve their differences. Thus, ngano gives people a room for dialogue to solve their differences. (Mabasa, 2019)

PANORAIRWA MWANA WASHE MURANDA TERERA
This Shona proverb urges servants to listen carefully of the good ideas that the king says to his children. Everyone benefits from that wisdom and can be used to strengthen relations and sustain it through appreciation of **diverse cultural values and identities**. Shona people have relatives and friends in the Diaspora who may bring new ideas which can be used to easy challenges through importation of goods and ideas or just the direct financial investment like the homelink initiatives that the country has embraced in order to develop the country. However not all ideas from outside home are good as innovation may also bring bad results as seen by the expensive cars, second hand cars which pollute theair space hence Tsuro in Redhiyo yaTsuro, said. "I heard nothing as I was coming from where the people live (**Handina chandanzwa nekuti kunogara vanhu ndiko kwandanga ndiri**)."

NGANO ZHINJI DZINOTANGA PANOPERERA SARUNGANO
Fortune (1982) said story endings reveal how adaptive tales are. Story tellers ends the tales with, "**Ndipo pakaperera sarungano** (That is where the storyteller ended), **Ndipo pakafira sarungano** (And then the storyteller died), **Ndipo pakagumira Sarungano** (That is where the storyteller ended), **Ndipo pakamwira nhondwa sarungano** (That is where the storyteller choked and died by drowning), **Ndiko kufa kwasara rungano** (And so they died and the story remained). Mabasa (2019) extends where Fortune ended on the discussion about tale endings positing that it is the Sarungano who dies but story remains, Furthermore arguing that this allows the new storyteller to look around on what issues need to be addressed so that they can be the new sources of the tale relevant to the new generation in order to address the challenges in real time. Mabasa's assertion set the new storyteller on an innovative

23

threshold demanding the new storyteller to fit into the life of the particular generation, using the available technology, recording new developments in the community in which the story or issues are to be stored or tackled. The researcher also notes that the old tales are the footprints which provides the new storyteller with the framework and structure of a folktale but still for the student to be relevant, one should find their new footing by branching out of the forerunners shaping their own and following the new dreams as demanded by their situation as they actively participate in learning important aspects of their culture (Ngugi wa Thiong'o 1987). This flexibility in Shona storytelling therefore allows audience to actively participate as backing vocalists or in form of asking questions that the storyteller answers or throws back to the audience to answer thereby disrupting the storytelling process in both time and the structure of the tale depending on the audience to which the story is being told to.

IMPLICATIONS

Folktales are an act of showing bravery, where the little expected results shock the most expected results. It is the chronicles of how giant ideas like Goliath are slain by the small David mighty ideas. Tales can be said to be documentation of events of their time that were recorded orally by our ancestors hence Mabasa refer to them as newspapers of the time they were told of the events that would have happened and as a result some stories died because they were not timeless but others survived because they were timeless. In this regard, most hard news stories survive only the day they are published but deeply analyzed feature stories survive generations after generations hence the relationship of Gudo and Tsuro in Shona tales is like deeply analyzed stories that can fit in every situation in any generation. This is qualified by storytelling functions of mediating and transmitting of knowledge and information about culture, world views morals, values, norms, and what the future is expected to be (Ngugi wa Thiong'o 1982). Not to say that all feature stories that find space in the new generation are relevant to these times without reorientation, Mabasa's argument that storytelling was like a newspaper holds water as it speak along innovative ideas therefore immediately correct the misbehaviour of the people in the community in which they were told,. And a newspaper is regarded as a primary source for a people's history. So, tales were also used to record our historical events that would have changed the people's way of life in what Chinyowa (2001) attests that storytelling is a way beyond just a source of pleasure, the story aids in sharpening the people's creativity and imagination, shaping their way of presenting themselves before others, training their intellect and regulating their emotions, attitudes and feelings.

Through most of his tales, Mabassa oozes with innovative ideas that conserve the structure of storytelling skills and indigenous values and norms. His tales is a clear demonstration that Shona knowledge moves with times and document contemporary developments. Mabasa (2014) argues that if the same tales were used in the past to solve societal problems what can surely stop them from solving our myriad problems today?

If we put Tsuro naGudo in silos, we risk presenting them as they were in the time of Mbuya Nehanda and our children will not find them appealing. If we really cared about Tsuro naGudo, we would be rebranding them so that they are relevant to young people today. (Mabasa, 2014).

In all his efforts Mabasa (2019) wants to bring back the shona people to their right senses or to where Achebe said 'where the hail stone started hitting us' and find the way out of the problems facing them hence he says;

Tales are not mere stories but they inspire you to think, they give you knowledge, they give you an understanding of expected morals in your society and how to live well with others in your community, they teach you to be a storyteller, they give you confidence to speak before a people, away from an individual worlds that we have constructed for ourselves in our ears through earphones that deprives us of conversations. So it is an effort to bring back people together again reminding them that a person is a person because of others around them not because of their electronic gadgets. (Mabasa, 2019)

CONCLUSION AND RECOMMENDATIONS

This study found out that Shona storytelling always moves with times, it has never been static as is proven by various proverbs which point to the urgency of the Shona people in its desire to move with times. Mabasa's critics therefore are hugging kusafunga as they seem to ignore the urgency in Shona knowledge systems' urge and instruction to move with times, be innovative and embrace change. Mabasa has managed to adapt to changing firesides through his embrace of the new technology in his bid to find audiences where they socialise in this fast moving life of this modern day. Shona indigenous knowledge systems therefore have ever been supporting innovative ideas as a way of sustaining the development of storytelling hence Mabasa is therefore not a sinner. Mabasa is not an irresponsible cultural dissident. Mabasa is not a rebel bent on mutilating Shona indigenous knowledge systems but a loyal Shona cultural ambassador taking Shona to the world the same way Tuku took Korekore to the world through Music. Mabasa is a faithful innovator of the Shona language whose aim is to prevent Shona storytelling from disappearing. Mabasa has taken upon himself to not only talk about the innovative use of storytelling in solving our contemporary challenges but has gone further into putting to practice by leading the way in showing what should be done with Shona indigenous knowledge systems. Mabasa is not just a speaker but a doer whose hunger for the preservation of Shona language extends the same journeys, paths capturing new territories that the ancestors because of change of eras did not traverse. Instead of vilifying him Shona knowledge conservationists should embrace him and complement his efforts to take Shona storytelling to the global sphere. Mabasa's innovative skills saw him attending the Third Razavi International Storytelling Festival in Iran as far back as 2012. What this means is that his stories has been seen speaking to the people of this time's needs locally, regionally and internationally therefore they are relevant and thus sustainable. Moreover this chapter has observed that, Shona storytelling is a long life travel by a bus that the old storytellers disembark upon arriving at their destinations as the bus is filled by new storytellers who also disembark when they reach their

26

destination and leave their seats to yet another generation of storytellers thereby illustrating that Shona knowledge systems encourage urgency, embrace change, advocate for change, borrow ideas therefore it is not stagnant but a flowing river being strengthened by its tributaries.

However this study observed a noticeable increase in the utilisation of indigenous foodstuffs in the modern day, increased campaigns to utilise indigenous diseases fighting and prevention methods, consumption of indigenous foods, growing of indigenous grains and as a way of mitigating the effects of climate change and non-communicable diseases therefore it recommends that since masawu, tsvubvu, mazhanje, nyii, mutetenerwa, and mahewu have found their way into the modern market system, storytelling should take them aboard in order to sustain their effects on the Shona society's health.

References:
Achebe, C. (1958). *Things Fall Apart*. Nigeria: William Heinemann Ltd.
Barnhart, C. L. and Barnhart, R. K. (1992) *World Book Dictionary*. Chicago: World Book, Inc.
Chinyowa, K. (2001). *"The Sarungano and Shona Storytelling: an African Theatrical Paradigm." Studies in*
        Theatre and Performance **21**(1): 18-30.
Constitution of Zimbabwe Amendment (No.20) 2013.
Dalton, M. and Stockil, C. (1987) Shangani Folk Tales. Harare:Longman.
Fortune, G. (1982) *Ngano Volume 11,* (collected by Mufuka, R 1972 & Edt Fortune), Mercury Press:
        Harare
----------------------(2010) *Oxford Advanced Learner's Dictionary*. New York: Oxford University Press.
Gbadegesin, S. (1984). *"Destiny, personality and the ultimate reality of human existence." Ultimate Reality*
        and Meaning **7**(3): 173-188.

Gombiro, P. (1985) *Tsuro Kanoshereketa*. Harare: Zimbabwe Children's Literature Foundation (ZCLF).

Grant, M. (1989). *School methods with younger children*. London: Evans Brothers Ltd.

Kunene, D. P. (1991). *Journey in the African epic. Research in African Literatures 22* (2): 205-223.

Mabasa, I. T. (2013) *Redhiyo yaTsuro*. Harare: Bhabhu Books.

Mabasa, I, T. (2013) *Behind my children's stories*. Harare: Zimbabwe International Book Fair

Mabasa, I. T. (2014) *Language teaching, the cultural dissident*. The Herald. Harare: Zimpapers. 29 July, 2014

Mabasa, I. T. (2016) *Chipo neChipopayi*. Harare: Bhabhu Books.

Mabasa, I. T. Mabasa releases folk tales. The Herald. Zimpapers. 17 April, 2017.

Mabasa, I. T. (2019) *Sarungano Ignatius Tirivangani Mabasa vanotandara naTinashe Muchuri vachitaura ngano*. munyori.com.

Mbara, V. (2017) Mabasa releases folk tales. The Herald. Harare: Zimpapers. 17 April, 2017.

Mkandla, P.N. (1974) *Abaseguswini lezothamlilo*. Harare: Longman Zimbabwe (Pvt) Ltd.

Mufanechiya, T. & Mufanechiya, A. (2015) *Teaching Chishona in Zimbabwe: A Curriculum Analysis Approach*. In The Journal of Pan African Studies, vol.8, no.8, November 2015. Masvingo: Great Zimbabwe University

Mungoshi, C. (1989) *Stories from a Shona Childhood*. Harare: Baobab Books (a division of Academic Books (Pvt) Ltd)

Mungoshi, C. (1991) *One Day, Long Ago: More Stories from a Shona Childhood*. Harare: Baobab Books (a division of Academic Books (Pvt) Ltd)

Mushava, S. (2016) *Masters and disruptive innovators*. The Herald. Harare:Zimpapers

Mushava, S. (2019) *Prison officer's runaway imagination*. The Herald. Harare:Zimpapers.

28

Muyambo (2016) *Indigenous Knowledge Systems: An Alternative for Mitigating HIV and AIDS in Zimbabwe.* Harare: *Alternation* 23,2 (2016) 289 – 308 ISSN 1023-1757

Ngugi wa Thiong'o (1982). *Devil on the Cross (English translation of Caitaani mutharaba-Ini).* Nairobi, Kenya, Heinemann Educational Books (East Africa) Ltd 1980.

Ngugi wa Thiong'o (1987). *Decolonising the Mind: The Politics of Language in African Literature.* Harare: Zimbabwe Publishing House (ZPH).

Vambe., M. T. (2001). *Orality and Cultural Indentities in Zimbabwe.* Gweru, Zimbabwe: Mambo Press.

Wasamba, P. (2018) A *ZIBF Indaba with a difference.* Harare. The Patriot. The Heritage.

UNESCO. (2019) International *Year of indigenous languages 2019.* Official website for the International Year: https://en.iyil2019.org/ accessed on 19 June 2019.

Zimbabwereads (2012) *Ignatius Mabasa to go to Third Razavi International Storytelling Festival in Iran.* https://zimbabwereads.org/news/ accessed on 15 May 2019

A Special Place
Matthew K Chikono

Two years after the Chimurenga war ended my older sister, Tilda, came back home. It was almost seven years since she had sneaked away from the house during a November stormy night. My mother had started believing that, somehow, she had found a way to join the freedom fighters across the border in Mozambique, and by the grace of the lord, she had perished with thousands of other young people fighting for the liberation of Zimbabwe. It was a lie of course, she didn't want to believe what my father said was a disgrace to the family; Tilda, the daughter of a strict village pastor and his wife who was a primary school headmistress, had ran away to Salisbury to indulge in wantonness and debaucheries only offered by the city. Well it didn't matter much though; she had finally come back home. She didn't come alone though, a six-year-old boy was in her tow.

They couldn't accept a bastard in their home, my parents said.

In a way they were right, Takura, for that was his name, was not ours to keep but his father's family. My father could not fathom the idea of keeping his daughter's embarrassment for the world to sneer and laugh at, that would have been rubbing salt to a fresh wound. I couldn't imagine what would happen to the pastor's famous fornication preaching in the village, if the pastor's own daughter could not follow them then who would? Before she had even unpacked her bags, the pastor was ready to kick her outside of his house. Tilda sobbed.

In their scaling of their daughter's morality they almost left out the most important thing; Takura was their grandson and my nephew too. His father might have been one of the countless men my sister associated with at the shebeen she worked at in the city or maybe one of the boys who had ran away to die in the war, my sister wasn't sure. She was a whore who would burn in hell, my mother did not mince her words. Tilda wept.

Shedding tears for the plight of her child was something that made me believe Tilda genuinely loved her son and it struck my eyes and my mother's heart. The headmistress would not sit and watch her daughter kneeling on the ground waiting for whatever life was about to through at her. She joined her daughter in rolling in the mud begging the Lord's servant to soften his stance. The husband loved the wife too much to refuse her of anything, he agreed for the sinner to sleep in the house for the night until a permanent solution could be found the following day. Tilda left.

Unlike the first time, she had the courtesy of leaving a note explaining that she had been called back to work and she would come back in few days to see her son. Few days turned into few weeks and my parents were already planning to go to the city and dump the little brat wherever its mother was participating in promiscuous behaviour. Before they could pack it off, they took a final look at the boy. Although he wore oversized khaki shorts and no shoes, it was apparent that he was the fragile type, so thin that he would shatter if squeezed too hard. His well patched and even torn shirt exposed his smooth and handsomely dark skin. That was his only clothes. His huge black hair added an inch to his short height. His tiny nose and ears matching his small mouth with an adorable huge smile. And his eyes, sometimes I wonder if they only kept him because of his eyes.

At six Takura had neither seen the comeliness of moon nor the horror or the summer sun. His eyes could open but all what he has endured since birth was darkness. Unlike some children of his age, colours were a myth to him and the beauty of the night sky a legend to his pretty little ears. Takura's mother had never said anything about his blindness, she had just pretended that everything was well, but I knew my sister, it must have been tiring to ignore the difference.

The first thing I ever gave him was a walking stick. I picked up a perfectly straight wooden stick along the road, tied a tiny steel metal on one end and some cloth on the other end to make a comfortable handle. I didn't know if it was of any use but every blind person, I ever saw seemed to possess it. Later I was glad I did, after some few weeks of

31

practice he was able to travel a bit further from our house. Without the need to crawl or kneel after few steps the stick gave him a huge smile and a little freedom.

The little freedom of walk allowed him to go and look for friends further than our homestead. This is how he discovered the other use of the stick, assaulting his mates. Believe me when I say he wasn't a bully he only beat up those who used to laugh or mock him about his eyesight. I was proud of him, at first, but it later turned out that he was really a bully. Once or twice every other week, an adult from the village would come to complain to the pastor about his grandson's hitting their child. It became a norm that caused the grandfather to specifically ask me to take away the stick from Takura.

No, I told the grandfather, Takura needs the stick to walk and defend himself out there it's a cruel world for boys like him.

The pastor did not understand, he believed in holy love. He wanted Takura to take everything in because his rewards and blessings were heavenly. He tried to teach him about love and doing good to your neighbour, but it was already too late.

Takura and I used to stroll around the village together a lot that people started to believe he was my son. I encouraged them; I didn't find any fault in it. It didn't sound strange when he started calling me father, although for a while I had to explain repeatedly to my then girlfriends the existence of this motherless child. The sight of us walking hand in hand was so touching that some villagers offered us some coins. We took them bought ourselves some sweets, we didn't need their pity, little acknowledgement that Takura was like another child was enough.

He was like other children, Takura was. In our happy hours I used to teach him to whistle and play a drum. He was way better at singing and dancing than me I later learnt. He was afraid of water and I had to give up teaching him swimming because he couldn't let go off my hands when we were in the water. It wouldn't come as a surprise that ploughing and herding cattle wasn't easy for him but shearing nuts, packing, and storing maize was something the entire family left him to take care of on his own.

My mother wanted me to teach him how to play music, that way when he was old enough, he would make noises and tunes in streets and buses to warranty handouts from strangers. If I had been holier then I would have just prayed for a better future for him. My mother was kind enough to teach him to wash his own clothes, I do believe she did it so that she could not touch the filthy blind bastard's underwear. I don't even know if my father acknowledged his presence at his homestead. Tilda never asked about him and I am glad he never asked of his mother too, I want to believe that he saw in me an uncle worth be a father. A kind family he deserved.

It has been two years since I last saw the boy. My father, the dear old pastor, sold one of his prized cows to send Takura to the special school that cater for his needs. The school is in the city and I can't afford to visit him. I couldn't tell if it was out of love or the desire to get rid of the bastard that drove my father to do such selfless act, but I am glad he did. Now I can hope that there is a future and place for him in the society we live in. Despite being in the same city with his mother they have never met or talked since he was six. We regularly send each other letters, although his have become less frequent than ever. He will find a person kind enough to read and write his letters, Takura claims. It doesn't matter, I always tell him, you will always have a special place in my life.

Reject or Accept Everything
Tendai Rinos Mwanaka

The only route to real freedom or the truth is to accept everything or to reject everything. Reject you know everything, reject there is a God, reject all religions, reject love, reject everything like an atheist, but go beyond atheism and reject yourself. Come to nothingness. That's the truth zone, that's true freedom. I didn't say come to sad nihilism (I didn't say delete yourself). After all everything is an opinion. Just because the majority have enforced it as the truth doesn't mean it's not an opinion. Go back and find out where it all started. It was an opinion. Even mathematically speaking there are instances where 1 plus 1 doesn't equate to 2. The truth is we adapt, we evolve, we live (survive). We are never sure. That's why systems decay and new systems come up to build on previous systems that have run their course and failed to stay the test of time. We are just instances in time, fractured pieces flying and winnowing in time's vastness

Or we can alternatively (or at parallel) accept everything. Accept there is a God, Accept heavens and earth, accept there is love, accept the human condition, and accept your religion and every other religion. Accept he is gay, accept he has children, and accept he doesn't want to get married, accept your nothingness. If you only think just because you are a Catholic and that its the only true religion. If you think you are a Judaist and that its the only true religion, if you think you are a Buddhist and that its the only true religion, you are a liar. That's not true or it's just a sad half-truth. The moment you believe that religion of yours as the truth believe every other religion as the truth, accept everything. Why would you dispute the same God's creations or different Gods' creations. He never created a single thing before so why do you want to think your religion alone is the only one true. I know you can commandeer God and go about dictating what he said or did not say and call it the truth, but the only true god is the Truth, and the only truth is everything or nothing

Poetry

STOP TORMENTING ME IN MY SLEEP DAMBUDZO!
Tinashe Trymore Munengwa

You deplete my rest
And haunt me all night long
Like incessant heavy down pours
Pouncing and hissing on the dry grasslands of the savannah

In the middle of my sleep
Your laughter rattles my verse
And I hear your voice
Ripping through my bedroom walls
Like the sound of breaking clay pots
As you appear in my dreams
Gobbling every line that I cook
Like a crocodile munching a crowd of healthy flies

My friends suspect that I write like you Marechera
You puffed eccentric aroma to art
And I sniffed into your writings
Through the muzzle of my own works
Like morsels of cocaine fleeting through the nostrils
Of a helpless drug addict

Conspicuously, your bohemian spoors
Precipitates the bull of my mind
Your droppings radiate poetic ghosts
In a kraal which we share an intimate relationship
Some of my verses are cumulonimbus clouds
In which you're the condensation nuclei
Your artistry marinates my soul with creativity and abundance
And your vitriol whirls like some Cuban or Congolese waist
Gyrating in my lines and stanzas of Rumba and Dombolo

It electrifies my poetry to the bone marrow

Why are you then tormenting me in my sleep Dambudzo?
Are you bitter with venom?
That you vanished a few years before I appeared
Like dew in a hot October morning
Or as riotous angry smoke
Wafting through the horizons of the thin air

Do not fume at me, my cantankerous comrade
Perhaps it is you who rekindled in me
As a matchstick that ignites at dusk
Or like an apple that doesn't fall far from its mother
So am I to you my bountiful tree

As the clock ticks Mr Dambudzo Marechera;
The ozone layer continues to deplete rapidly
While new viruses naughtier than HIV fume with blossom
So...
Lease me a contract to construct my own art
Grant me wings so that I soar to the sky
And erect immortal history such that when the floods come
Accompanied by earthquakes and volcanoes
To corrode time better than viruses, acids and nuclear bombs
My poetry will not be defecated
In the urinals of history

As that grandfather clock continuously revolves
I will inevitably be a souvenir to history;
A special artefact to antiquity as you
When that time comes;
Let these last beleaguered lines
Cemented in this fertile stanza
Be the ultimate demise of your torture:

Stop tormenting me in my sleep Dambudzo!
x

THIS SICK SOCIETY
Tinashe Trymore Munengwa

Today is that day I'm disgusted
Let my soul vomit this rampant contamination of my society
Scores of incurable diseases haunt us
Viruses with razor teeth have germinated
While youths mistreat drugs
My generation misuses alcohol, boncleer* and dagga
Our fathers penetrate everywhere
They entice and rape their own daughters
Like hen smacking through the yoke of its own eggs
My society has decomposed,
Grown men eat unripe fruits
While our own mothers walk half naked
The boys have found pleasure in fornicating, stealing and killing
As hoodlums with attires of justice are tainting the society
With conspicuously stinking corrupt tendencies
Their duty is to fortify us against injustice
Yet they openly exchange justice with the dollar
Even the opium of the society is being used avariciously
Hypocrites who masquerade with the holy book
Have mushroomed like fungi
This has disintegrated the social fabric of my society
As immorality is now rampant
And dances in the atmosphere as carbon dioxide
Even nature riots:
Floods, drought, earthquakes, volcanic eruptions and global warming
All have come to reside on our planet,
At the lap of this civilization like ink on paper
And scoffs at humanity

Alas, half a million have died of the novel Corona virus
In less than six months
As death herself is triumphing
What is left below this heartless and venomous sky
Is a very sick society!

*A cough syrup

IN THE GHETTO
Tinashe Trymore Munengwa

Under the hot African sun
Is the stinking ghetto
Where houses are analogous to a squatter camp
Kissing and fondling is rampant
Like HIV and AIDS in the red blood cells
Older boys squeeze and fondle
The erect breasts of virgins drenching them
Like armpits swamped by perspiration
On a scorching October afternoon

This happens in broad daylight
At the periphery of the defecated wetlands,
Adjacent to the rotten location,
In the sewage-infested and decomposed pathways,
In council excreted and foul-smelling toilets,
In squalid and decayed bedrooms
Literally everywhere!

These teenage girls scream deafeningly
As several long black thorns penetrate

Through the soft tissue of their feet
Like police spikes perforating the soft tyres
Of a kombi in the CBD of Harare
Better than a hot knife through the bums of frozen margarine
These under-aged girls and illegitimate mothers scream deafeningly
And have been poked countless times
While the poor lads spit weak seeds inside their contaminated wombs

What have you…?
Teenage pregnancies
Sexually transmitted diseases;
The deadly syphilis and gonorrhoea
HIV and AIDS
Tuberculosis and cancer
Orphans and street urchins
Juvenile prisoners
Proliferating drug abusers
Unparalleled unemployment
Adolescent burglars
Young and old prostitutes
Yet fake prophets are mushrooming like bacteria
As the craving for demos prolong
Among a disgruntled populace
In the ghetto

Sunset
Chiedza Dziva

In the whisper of the wind I'm lost.
My heartbeat in perfect synchronisation with the whistle
Of the trees as they sway away.
The last happy flocks fly away to their nests to nestle
But I remain to paint, with the colours of the demise of day,
my world that's gone grey.
The last strands of gaudy light disappear
Paving way for a serene darkness.
Heaven on this twilight is near
Filling my heart with gladness.
Surely I know now the remedy to my despair;
A dose of the setting sun slowly does away with my fear.

FORGOTTEN DRUM

Everjoice Marwa

Out in the cold
I am all alone dumped and forgotten
I live behind the granary.
No one seems to remember the good times we had together.
The hide on my head, dry and cracked.
Sad and filled with melancholy, l remember my promise to the sacrificial bull.
That l will give his children joy.
The young and the old, will always be united by my rhythm
We used to have fun at rainmaking ceremonies and all celebrations alike.
Now am no longer needed, weather forecasts ursuped me.
They say technology has advanced , and irrelevant l have become.
They say things of the past, must stay in the past.

So in their past l stay.
Still clutching onto the good memories.
The joy we had during our union, from my memory l will never erase.
With pain heartbreak and sadness, like a ditched lover, l lament my demise.

LETTER FROM DIASPORA
Everjoice Marwa

I am sorry it took so long to contact you
I just want to say l love you
Your face is an unremovable stamp in my heart honey
I could see no one else other than you wish this letter is accompanied by
something else but am sorry my love l haven't found any job yet.
The grass is not always as green as it seems from that side
 All those talks about having chicken everyday, going to KFC to dine
there, wearing Nike, Puma and Adidas,
Am sorry l haven't come across that life ever since l came here
Yesterday l went to bed on an empty stomach.
The other day l spent the whole day on one vetkuk
They call them magwinya here
 Don't feel so sad after reading this letter
I am doing everything possible to find a job
But without proper documents its not so easy
Since the home affairs police are always breathing down my neck.
I am going to the market everyday
Not your usual market where you buy vegies
Its where we advertise ourselves for work.
Some are picked and some are not
Unfortunately my love, luck seems so far from me right now
But don't be disheartened, one day am gonna be picked and score a
R100.
That is the daily wage for manual labour here
Wish l could earn more and send you the sandals you loved so much.
I am sorry l cannot bring you here as promised honey
I am sorry l have failed you
But l won't give up
The hope to see you again keeps me going.
It gives me the strength to face another day

I hope this letter finds you well
I LOVE YOU.

Heartache, Heartbreak and Unfulfilled Desire.
Michael Perseus

We bled so much we turned the world into a horrific landscape we could
not stomach,
And the only way we saw fit to live in the dystopia we created was to use
the blood we spilled to pen songs to our broken hearts, and etch poetic
inscribings for our worthless husks of a soul;
And from that liquid life we drew, from our shattered bones and
wounded bodies: filled with heartbreak, heartaches and everything desire
could not give,
We wrote something beautiful;
Something that could distract us from the ugly truths that come with this
sadness we suddenly found ourselves gifted with,
It was our own cosmic reset, our own form of redo
"And perhaps," we thought, "we would not have to suffer the memory of
what we once were; perhaps we could begin anew."
I have stopped finding romance or beauty in heartbreak,
But I still cling to the fool's dream; that if I write what I feel, I won't have
to suffer from what I hide anymore.

Navigating the middle
Michael Perseus

Ask me about all my insecurities and I will tell you they all arose from the
overwhelming desire for identity,
That my lowered self-esteem rose from being told I would never be
enough, and being cursed for being too much,
And having a heart, wrapped and layered in thick scar tissue from
trusting too easily, and having a double-edged sword plunged into me;
the one who removed his armour, the one who wanted to let himself be
known,
I guess you could say I was water to a rich man; bland and tasteless and
not what he wanted,
And simultaneously I was the waters of the typhoon; endless and
monstrous and everything that could drown, all you hold dear;
Ask me about my insecurities and I will tell you it was a constant struggle;
navigating the path between being too much and not being enough.

Love and Healing
Michael Perseus

I love you the way I love the smell of old books in an endless library,
with wonder and eyes filled with dreams,
I have loved you the way I loved dancing in the rain; with ecstatic joy and
unhindered self-ease, content in the moment and unburdened by worry,
I will love you the way I love myself, with trembling heart and an eternal
wish, my heart has been shattered and I don't have all its pieces
But I know no matter how far away each piece will love you the same,
with no fear and with its all,
And, perhaps, loving you will heal what love once broke.

HONESTY
Kumbirai Farai Constance Kupfavira

Overrated, over emphasized
Never lived, never will

Standstill\ Zombies
Kumbirai Farai Constance Kupfavira

Lights on, pose, camera
Hold it right there
Keep your chin up
Look to the left
Breathe in and hold
Nice, perfect
Will take two more
You can relax\what different are we with a zombie
Automated to one function
If they even exist?

You need to dress up
I mean wear a brand
You are beautiful
Sorry only with a little touch ups
Glam, perfection, model
A certain particular inch
Accredited by those who want
Need you to be their own
Doll, patent, image
A dimension drawn with accuracy
What difference are we with a
Exclamation, a standstill?

Right there perfect look
Glossy lips, awesome calves
Toned legs, bold looks
Magnetic eyes
An illustration of an image
Not perfect but constructed in the mind

To bring you at your feet
Amazed, perplexed
Yes you are there
At a standstill

SHADOWS
Kumbirai Farai Constance Kupfavira

We try to run away from
But it sticks with us
Depending on the obliteration of the moon and sun
Shadows narrates our story
The only permanent dents of our lives

Netsai's song
Tafadzwa Chiwanza

Darkness crawls from the abyss
Forming a pact with the angry night,
To keep me far from Netsai's arms.

A monstrous wall of moist darkness;
The air I breathe when eyes see her not
Flooding my lungs with acidified gases.

Words are thistles pricking my tongue,
But I feel the urge to sing one last time
A song only the raving wind can carry

I can see beyond the veil now,
A hand beckons and I must heed,
But to the wind my last wishes I trust;
Let Netsai know I was always made of dust!

Camera captured chaos

Tafadzwa Chiwanza

Cameras captured the carnage
As salvos of grenades exploded.
Terrible terror tearing flesh loudly,
Like it were the veil in the temple:
Made the maddened men run,
So fast that flesh tore from their limbs.

At the sooty heart of the chaos,
Another man stood still with jaws ajar
Gawking at his shadow which did sit,
Refusing to run from the chaos.

From moaning to mourning
Tafadzwa Chiwanza

Scrubbing for scrambled words
to scribble my way to immortality.
I've found life's chair to be too small
for both partitions of my buttocks.

Extract words from this mine,
And leave heaped sand as evidence,
Like a discarded condom dripping semen:
A witness to pleasures, then horrors,
That oscillated from moaning to mourning.

THAT SONG AGAIN
Edwell Zihonye

Its lyrics were penned underground.
The words cut into each other like swords,
Causing confusion in the ears.
Far away from the citadel of humanity
Civilisation is grazed and grated.
Our hustling is beyond description.
Feelings we've set aside for ages.
Our interaction is a platform for lunacy,
A programme to sell grime,
A plan to deodorize group insanity.
The melody inspires indescribable error.
It's that song again!
When I hear it again,
My muscles freeze.
Incidents, years-old, come back.
Cruel visions return with vengeance.
I see the children walking away.
Peers are peering at the distant horizon.
Colleagues walk with drooping shoulders,
Their abused backs hunched.
When I hear that song again,
A dark cloud envelops my path.
It's that horrid song again!
I'm forced to dance to a non-existing tune ...

I MOURN
Edwell Zihonye

I mourn the death of industry,
The smell of human sweat,
Hands gripping real machines,
Eyes on the hectares under crops,
Savouring the damp summer soil,
Birds encouraging the sower,
Human and vehicular traffic conversing,
Movement with a common purpose.

I mourn the crippled courtesy
Dumped at the crossroads.
Renowned kindness has been split,
Fellowship exiled in the wastelands
And accountability severed in public.

I mourn the abandoned language,
Replaced by streams of invectives and insults.
Corrupted young mouths just blubber.
Tender brains mangled and scattered.
We witness calumny at sunrise,
The birth of short cuts and shady deals!

I mourn the demise of human feelings.
Communality is on rocky ground,
Collaboration swept away by a flooded river.
Potholes and gullies are born in droves.
I mourn, ceaselessly,
The sprouting of institutional anarchy.

IT'S NOT TRUE
Edwell Zihonye

I have discovered, to my horror
That it's not true ...!
Names do not come from big gifts,
Small amounts don't scare away laughter,
Tiny bits don't invite the mournful.
A smile does not mean happiness.
It's scary when you know,
It's pitiful when you see,
It's despairing when you hear,
It's disheartening when you feel,
It's nauseating when you smell,
And it's pathetic when you touch.
I will divulge the secret load of my heart.
The heart is a distraught organ,
Abandoned in no-man's land.
Where did we go wrong?
When did we follow a detour?
Why do we call trivia an important deed?
It's misnomer of the worst kind.
We visit even at unholy hours.
We dread inquiries into our affairs.
We dream of great responsibilities.
We dredge love with sprinkles of emotions.
We believe too much in inequality.
No one pays heed to another's pleas.
Along sullen streets, we trudge
But appear to be happy.
We traverse miles of desolate terrain
But seem to enjoy it.
It's not true, I say!

All is a drudgery.
All is a tumultuous existence.
We yearn for the return of order.
Confused, weary and agitated,
We plod on our way.
It's not true that we are happy!

The Waters of Lost Things
Troy Da Costa

There is a pool where I grew up. No one knows how deep it is, the waters are so black you cannot see the bottom and the mud is so thick anything lost in it would never be found.

The kids there live in this pool their feet sinking in the mud, and they laugh and joke because they're together and play silly games. But the mud, it keeps them in there, holding them down, and everything is in the mud.

The neglecting parents, the poor education, the angry policemen, the corrupt officials, drugs, alcohol, promises, the potential employer who has no faith in them because they grew up in this mud. They're all there holding them down, part of the mire.

And the kids they can see the good things all around them, they can see the fields of wildflowers that offer freedom, they look to the stars, try as they may they can never reach them.

Somehow this is their fault; this is their choice to be here, but they were born in this mud, they were born in this skin, they were born in this dark water.

And what do you think happens when one of these kids wades ashore, to join the civilised. There is no pat on the back, no "Well done," because he's still covered in mud, if anything "they" would do all in their power to push him back into those waters and hope he disappears never to be seen again.

There is a pool where I grew up and there are thousands of us yet still those are the loneliest waters you'll ever find.

The Spider and the glass
Troy Da Costa

The windows burnt with morning fire, so I moved across the table like a spider and poured the poison from the glass. The TV whistled and hummed with stars. All I saw was the dull ache that rots; death, hate and putrid states of being.
I must leave this place.

So, I moved across the table like a spider through the broken door of my dreams and into the joyless sunlight. With fresh pain to sell the man, I placed my heart on a train that never stopped, to a desk that sounded like hungry teeth grinding. And as the moments beckoned, delighting in my misery I set my pen to the ground. I dug the grave of a thousand words, and they paid in drops of my own blood.
I must leave this place.

Night crept and broke the heat with cool suits and the promise of love. So, I moved across the table like a spider, through the ice that formed. Freedom stood open chested and beaten with the cat. I licked her face for just one sweet taste, but her tears were acid and her skin began to flake.
I sat to figure the situation; what had just begun? At the other end, the liquid stood waiting to be consumed.

I must leave this place.

So, I moved across the table and poured the poison from the glass.

The shadow of Mummering
Troy Da Costa

The cold hard water snaps my face, this is how I dream. In shades of shooting stars across black winds where once stood rocky children. And those black winds call across the continents to where we sleep in beds made of hands. Hands that snap their fingers to watch us dance with scornful eyes. The eyes of unforgotten gods, resentful of my dream to be alive. I wake and fall from one unbearable moment to the next; to right the lives of unmet generations begging my mercy. A mercy that does not belong to me. A mercy that will never come. Through this turbulence some live fearlessly but I seek the comfort of ignorance.

THE BLISS FROZE
Wilson Waison

The bliss froze
It's yet another winter spell
With barren thoughts it evokes in me,
It's frost biting like the stubborn jaws of a lion
I can feel the might, breaking bones
Yes I am a victim
Left gnashing from the seizure
Of what was a family.

In these torrid times,
I starve for love and affection
And the winter still brew it's blizzards
That pierce through all that remains
Yes it's the winter which saw
Mom and Dad separate
Another winter I lost a lad
Yes, a hope of a nephew devoid,
She lost her son to the merciless demons.

Double fold it's two years gone
And the separation harshly felt
I bare the pain and it's burden
    over my weak shoulders
Yet the load became heavier with each day
And the grinning clock
    that hang loosely from the wall
Keep on smiling at me...

THEY CAME LONE NIGHTS
Wilson Waison

They came lone nights,
Long days in distraught
Drowning in thoughts of what was
Till a breach of trust devoid;
   a jovial mood.
And cemented much hate and pain.

I tasted from a bitter fruit
Egged from a premature divorce
Cat fights we had grown to be used
Till that winter came
And termed shame upon us
Cracking bliss into fragments
Pieces of hate and agony splattered
And pierced through my fragile heart.

Sister left vulnerable
Devoured by the trauma;
   a sheep skinned hyena
Chewed her happiness in laughter
And I saw, incapacitated
We both got bruised in an effort
   to flee but reality...
Reality became a fantasy bubble bursting.

Alien
Kabelo Sithole

They didn't pick E.T. up

when he phoned home?

Did he move to

 Africa?

Did the Rain dance in

 Njelele, knowing he could

control the weather.

They worshiped

him as Divinity,

For health and strength

And daily

bread.

Perchance,

 he doesn't thirst for your

company,

Fulfilled by long walks

on beautiful streets.

Eternally seeking the next

 tree to hug,

At no time halting for the way

 you gaze at an outlander.

Perchance,

he pines for home,

He sees faces you'd never perceive

 in the clouds

by mean solar day

Shapes you can't figure

 in the constellations

by night.

Perchance,

he has to slap himself

 occasionally

And hold fast to a memory

To let him know

he is at no time

alone even though

he perpetually is.

Can you see him now?

 So tired of hearing,

 his finger say

'the number you have dialed

is unreachable, please try again later'.

Gnome
Kabelo Sithole

A garden gnomes day:

Drinking cups of morning sunshine

With a side dish of tender breeze

To spend days with grasshoppers

Contemplating the multiverse

Nights dining with stars

And a glass full of whatever Oblivion is having

The music in my head is called 'home'

In winter my favorite thing is to freeze

Weekends I awkwardly stare at passing shoppers

It's called freedom, this suspended animation, even behind bars

Seeing it is
Kabelo Sithole

Intermittent rain

I dance to your Melody

You lock me inside,

I swear I saw it.

She kissed the jacarandas,

Save some love for me

Let's Free the lillies!

That's what you demanded, right,

One icy winter.

Please, don't rush to work

drink some morning sunshine first

And a bird song sandwich

SWEETEST VOICE
Cosmas Tinashe Shoko

Her voice is just sweet like pineapple,
From the estuaries of my heart-- I smile,
I have found happiness,
She knows I am mesmerized,
I am in love with her voice,
A voice smooth and tender,
She arouse me to my deepest consciousness,
So stunned by the virtue of her voice,
Her voice, so sweet like red wine,
When I met her, I knew,
In my heart, I knew,
I had to tell her,
She knows yes, she knows!
I am in love with her voice!

HOLD MY HAND FOR A DANCE
Cosmas Tinashe Shoko

Let's dance through the stars smile,
Come beloved; hold my hand for a dance,
Tonight you look majestic,
The decorum of your dress like red carpet shines,
The sassiness of your being like beauty epitomize,
I am intrigued by your free spirit,
Will you not shy me away?
I will kiss you through the night,
Let me humor with a glass of wine,
Come let us watch the evening stars together,
Sing songs of time,
For I have known you for some time,
You were there for me when I needed a friend,
Today is our date, come hold my hand,
Come to my arms beautiful,
Let's dance through sunrise!

Mass Grave
Mandhla A Mavolwane

War victims are buried in mass graves
Cramped, lifeless corpses on top of each other
There are no sorrowful hymns audible
No loud screams,
Just the sound of corpses piling up
Corona virus reintroduced mass graves
Land reserved for housing
Is now occupied by corpses.
Who declared war on planet earth?
Should we listen to conspiracy theories?
Should we listen to the religious men?
Or should we listen to the diplomatic men?
Can big bang theorists also argue?
Because no one has the answer
Mass graves are all over the planet
Prime time news is scary like a horror film.
Victims are inflating alongside the Zimbabwean currency.
There are no contraceptives for this virus
Even my pen is sneezing and coughing
Because the ink is dripping like mucus
And these words will lead it to a mass grave.

Trials and tribulations
Johannes Mike Mupisa

Theirs are beautiful mornings,
To me its mourning,
While the fortunate moan in glory,
A day peppered with mercy,
While mine is spoiled in a mess,
Bullet proof vests and lucid breasts
High up the social order they feast,
Bragging about all the feats,
Burying the downtrodden under their feet,
The swollen feet testimony to defeat,
Defeat of the fight to eat, sleep and live,
Leave hunger and lice infested shelters,
Crowded like mice feeding on lies,
Peddled by the same potbellied fortunate few,
Like cats the multitudes mew,
Like mules they toil ,
For crumbs like ants they scramble,
They painfully smile at the tokens,
The impetus for change escalates each election,
The hope recedes post-election,
The elasticity of hope is exhausted,
The pain gnaws and rigs into the psychology,
A troubled mind,
A mine of trials and tribulations

The Comrade
Johannes Mike Mupisa

Every 18th day of the forth month,
I reminiscence of the days in the bush,
Lice and ticks feeding on our thorn bruised skins,
The stenchy smell of our clothes engulfing our noses,
The smell of death hovering over our heads,
Each day was like a last furlong,
The whizzing of the helicopters circling over our heads,
Strafing the thickets smoke filling the air,
The blood thirsty mercenaries baying for our souls,
The hunger,
The thirst,
The dangerous animals,
The struggle was not a joke,
The victory not a serendipity,
We shook the metal yoke with force,
Unabashed am I about the independence,
A product of our toils,
I never regret this day,
A stop to white colonialism,
A start to black empowerment,
The journey as rocky as it may be,
The thrill of freedom is engraved on my heart,
Independence is INDEPENDENCE.

GOING HOME
Samuel Chuma

1
On that anthill yonder
They buried my umbilical cord
And returned me to dust
The day I was born

Before I could comprehend
Termites had already feasted
On my dumbfounded being
And excreted the remains
Into the latrine of oblivion

I roam this earth now
A bodied ghost thus drawn
To that dusty anthill
Where impatient termites
Await the main course
To the starter they tasted

2
Death smells like roses
At evening time
When the sun dies
In the ancient arms
Of steadfast mountains
That have seen it all
And refuse to mourn anymore

3

Does the housefly even know

Of livid human hatred
Compressed into atomized cans
That sneeze out genocide
To its kind and kindred?

Does it even care
When it shall have the last laugh
And subsist on the poor remains
Of its once mighty nemesis

Lying in sorry state
In some uncaring cemetery
Where the fallen mighty
Are trashed

4

Death smells like roses
Even when there are no noses
To pay homage to its scent
Which refuses to repose
When the whole world takes respite
But lingers to occupy
The gardens of the mind
With unrelenting presence

Like a curse.........

UPON SEEING A SHOOTING STAR
Samuel Chuma

We will sit and talk
About the trajectory
Of shooting stars
Whose source and destination
We know not
But whose brilliance for once
Illuminates our drabness
And gives us hope to dream
Of horizons yet unexplored
And universes still to be conquered

We will sit and wonder
If there indeed is milk
In the Milky Way
And why it remains uncurdled
By the rude intrusion of
Rockets and satellites
And the bold telescopic probes
Seeking to stare into the eye of God

MUSIC, LOVE & YOU
Samuel Chuma

Loving you is like
Dancing on a razor's edge
With feet unshod
Balancing like a trapeze artist
On the thin line
Demarcating loyalty and stupidity
Enslaved to pain and peril
But still waltzing away
Goaded on by the whipping
Of guitar string and piano wire
And the cruel thumping
Of the bass drum and congas
While the penny whistle
Ululates its glee

Despairing Mass
Haile Saize

Seduced mass soiled their hopes
Yet to reap mass graves
A harvest of thorns and thistles
That revealed the surviving cronies
As bloodthirsty forerunners who manipulated,
Monopolized
And butchered innocent poor souls
Souls melted in the pot of grotesque
And endless despair!

Country Folks Entangled In Dear Motherland
Haile Saize

My dear!
Do not raise your hand on my child
Crying to suck your tender breast
If he doesn't cry, he will starve to death
With diapers sunk in mess
Please undress him and redress him

My love!
Don't ever raise your voice
Or yell at our son's choice
For if you dare
He will turn into a prodigal
And our home will never embrace even strangers.

The roots
Jabulani Mzinyathi

That you do not see the foundation
Does not mean it is not there
That you see those branches
Does not mean there are no roots
Those stories of the past
A compass to the uncharted future

Those men left their villages
Where they were fathers
Respected by their wives
Respecting their wives in turn
Men uprooted from their courts

All kinds of taxes were due
Forced to labour in factories
Forced into domestic work
Family life was then fractured
Adjusting to an alien life style
These are the stories to forget

The stories they want us to forget
The tree must be uprooted
That is the derailment
Those men left their lives
Turned suddenly into bachelors
Living in prison cell like hostels

Men turned into tea boys
Delivering letters as post boys
Tending gardens as garden boys
Turned into spies against others

Those were the baas boys
The humiliation was total

Wrenched from their villages
To live in boys' *kayas*
Wrenched from their ways
Then told these were pagan
It was all termed *zvechibhoyi*
The beginning of perpetual boyhood
And you gleefully gobble that.

Zvechibhoyi is chiShona meaning that which is for a boy. Bhoyi is an
adopted word from the English word boy. In the eyes of the colonizer a
black man was always a perpetual boy.

Topsy Turvy
Jabulani Mzinyathi

To forever dwell
In the web of fear
The new creation
The covid 19 product
Cut off from others
The affection is severed
Bear hugs now outlawed
A litany of don'ts rising
Distancing hands from face
Natural impulses a taboo
Thoughts of nuclear warfare
A new weapon of mass destruction
Death and destruction in its wake

Deep chasms now evident
Biological warfare some say
The end of the World
Those of the apocalyptic side
The height of economic warfare
The world now torn apart
W.H.O threatened with death
Resources abruptly withdrawn
Humanity gripped by fear
The covid 19 virus exacerbating
That hunger virus on the rise
The ever present poverty virus
The World in dire need of healing

The cycle
Jabulani Mzinyathi

A chilly wintry night
Thick wintry darkness
The ominous night sounds
The darkest hour looming
No full moon out to play
A lustrous glow then sets in
Bird songs fill the air
Birds of all plumage
Each out to catch the worm
A new day has risen
The life cycle goes on

Gunyana ndokugunyana Gushungo
Chenjerai Mhondera

Regai vakuru varambire pazvigaro;
Kungoti ibvei ndiye tsvai!
Vanadzo nyanga kakanganwai zvenyu;
Vachamborarama.

Wako Muzenda munaGunyana akagunyana,
Iwe ukati ndiwo mwedzi wemadzimambo - wagunyanawo!

Kuneiko kwamunoti mose munongopitidzana?

Inga gore rino kwafa mikono;
Nzakera - mikandangari chaiyo;
Tuku, Ndunge, Dabengwa, newe Mugabe!

Ukati muridzi wembakumba mberi,
Murapi wako nechepapa
Wekureverana naye zviromokoto, kuseka nehurukuro dzemberi papa;
Twatwatwa; twako wasunga, ukati rangu harinyorwi rikadzimwa!
Rwendo mangwanani;
Rinozorova harozve nhongonya dzevakuru ini ndave kuna Zame!

Wakarida gutaro Gushungo,
Rawakaenda usina kana nekuoneka zvako!
Ndaiti tichaungana pazviteshi;
Naipo panhandare yadzo ndege;
Ukati inhema - chimhukutira ndirwo rwendo rwembwa!

Wakachekwa paiko zvausina kana nekuomba?
Wakabayiwa jekiseni ripiko risina kukuporesaro!
Wakadyiwa neiko mhiriko?
Toti imhepo yemundege here - yaita urwere hukombe?

Taura Robert!

Translation by author

September Wrapover
Chenjerai Mhondera

Let elders overstay on the throne
For resignation signals departure (passing on).
Those on throne, forget if they shall depart any time sooner

Your former deputy, Muzenda, left in September
And you took it to be a month of royal departure,
And so, you joined the fella!

What awaits there, that you go in such haste?

This year, rolled off Giants
It was Tuku, Ndunge, Dabengwa and now you Mugabe!
For you, the stage was well managed;
The musician ahead, to guest announce of your impending arrival,
Your medicine man with you
And a fellow comrade along with you, for eternal conversation
And so you vowed, you won't book only to cancel such a flight!
You decided a journey,
Early in tranquility and cold still of morning
before the sun could harass you

You loved that city, you of crocodile totem.
For you left for it, without bidding farewell.

I thought, we would gather terminus,

And even at international airports,
But you said, not this time!

Where did they cut you, that we heard not of your wail?
Was it a medical fault?
What fate befell you in such a distant land?
Shall we say, they are setbacks and upsets from the plane?
Tell, Robert! We want to know

afurika yedu!
Chenjerai Mhondera

handidi afurika
yakashama,
isina matyira
afurika isina kupfeka

afurika
matongo, ini handiidi -
isina chidziro zvese nedenga
afurika inoti
denga harinokupfurirwa
chidzirowo hachina kunamwa

handidi afurika
isina kuvhurika.
afurika yakambanywa
isinopamhama

afurika
isingavhurike
inoti chinguri
yakavharwa,
inongogomera ichiti
"apa pangu, nepapa!
mabayo! chipfuva! muviri kurwadza!
ndangariro!
nhamo! urombo! nzara! kushayiwa chokudya!"

handide afurika, gevha
inonyura poto,
inopukuta pukuta muromo, seisinokumbodya
inodya usiku, vamwe vavete,

yomukurovera bembera, seisinokumbodya.

handide afurika, isinokupangwa,
nekurongeka.
afurika, inomukira kumakwato;
afurika isingarime, kuti idye ichiguta

handidi afurika, yakachoboka,
yakapfeka zvigamba nemarengenya;
isingadye ichiguta

iyo afurika, torai henyu!
timene tigare,
timire,
tigosimba,
tigoreva,
tigovaka,
tigozendemura
afurika yatinoda
yemarudzi ose -
iyo isingasarudzi marudzi,
iyo afurika, imba yakavakwa
padombo, pagomo
afurika yako neni,
afurika yedu
afurika inoponisa
afurika inopundutsa
afurika inoruramisira,
afurika ine maguta,
afurika yakapamhama
kuti iwe neni tose tikwane

Translation by author

our afurika
Chenjerai Mhondera

I don't like this *afurika*
undressed
and fearlessly this heartless

afurika
the ruins, disgusting;
unwalled and roofless

afurika
not wise up -
tight, and not that flexible!

afurika,
that opens up not to fresh breath and air -
and gear to go.
oh such *afurika*, disgusting!
ever in groans;
pointing to own infirmities and inflamation of bones,
poverty, hunger, droughts and war.
oh no, i don't like this *afurika!*

i don't like *afurika*, dishonest
that steals from a pot due to serve everyone full;
afurika, pretentious
afurika with elements that wake to feed, others asleep
and conceal evidence that they have fed.

I don't like *afurika*, a rebel off roots
and disorganised;

afurika, that wakes to beg,
afurika, that doesn't embrace need to grow and feed self
afurika, broke -
vying in patches and rags.
afurika, sinning against own sufficiency;
afurika, that feeds but draws no satisfaction what it feeds on.

such *afurika*, conceal from my face!
for together, let's sit,
stand - firm;
talk,
build
and mould, *afurika* all want
for everyone to belong.
afurika, that is indiscriminately
afurika, built on a solid rock
on a plateau;
afurika, yours and mine
afurika, ours
afurika, saving
afurika, flourishing
afurika, just
afurika, well-fed
afurika, vastly great and accommodating
for you and i to fit and live in without difficulties

Takaringa
Fudzai Nyarumwe

Ko, seiko kundirasisa kudaro
Kundisiya ndiri pachena
Pasina kana chikwenzi chekuhwanda,
Wese andiona anodzungudza
Ko, ini ndini wekutanga here?
Hamuna kuti muchadzoka here?
Hezvo tande nenzira takaringa,
Kwakaenda imbwa ndokwakaenda tsuro.
Nanhasi ndakangogarira guyo sembwa
Ko, munorevereiko nhema?
Dai makanditaurirawo nguva ichiripo
Kuti muridzi wahwo ave kuhuda
Zvimwe ndaizogadzirira,
Mandigura kunorira Mai,
Asi ndingaiteiko
Kana vatongi vatonga?

Still expecting
Fudzai Nyarumwe
Translated by Oscar Gwiriri

Oh why betray me!
Setting me on bare ground
Where there is nowhere to hide,
Everybody sympathises with me
As if I'm the first one to befall this.
But, you promised to come back
I'm still gazing waiting for you.
You seem to have gone forever
And I'm patiently waiting for nothing
But, why lie to me after all?
Had you advised me in time
That time was calling for your life,
I would have otherwise emotionally prepared,
But see, you have hit me so hard Mom.
Anyway, what else can I do
When Heavens have ruled so?

Dambudziko
Simbarashe Chirikure

Tiri kushushikana vakuru,
Senzuma inoshaya chakadya nyanga dzayo.
Takawirwa nedambudziko guru,
Dambudziko risina kana mukare akamboona.
Mhepo huru nemafashamo emvura zvakatipura,
Takavarairwa zvikatirozva.
Takasara tisina pekuisa musoro kana chekubata.
Takafara tichiona vakuru vachisvika.
Vakatisimbaradza nemashoko.
Vakavimbisa rubatsiro,
Vachiti ratiwira iri ravawirawo.
Vaiti varikurwadziwa pamwe nesu.
Nhasi uno gore rapfuura,
Kwakaenda imbwa ndiko kwakaenda tsuro.
Takangoringa nzira tichiti rubatsiro rwuchauya.
Nhamo yatisvuura zvinosiririsa,
Mhepo, zuva nechando zvirikuita madiro aJojina nesu.
Zvipfuyo dzangove ndangariro.
Iyo nzara yadzika midzi zvino.
Hamheno tikapona gore rino.

Troubled
Simbarashe Chirikure
Translated by Oscar Gwiriri

We are quite disturbed
Like an ox pondering on its lost horns.
We encountered a daunting challenge,
Storms pounced on us unexpectedly
And left us stranded on strange ground.
We ululated to the attending authorities
Who consoled us and strengthened us,
Promising us social assistance and aid,
Comforting us that they were in our shoes.
Alas, a blank year has gone by now,
The promises are ashamedly empty.
In this merciless and avid poverty.
Whereby we're exposed to extreme conditions,
We've since forgotten about who were are,
Hunger has stricken us to intolerable levels
I wonder if we shall survive this stinging woe.

Kuzvidemba
Simbarashe Chirikure

Semhuru kumafuro, takarimbinyuka
Ndokudzana samambo Davhidha.
Takapembera nokufara,
Mifungo yedu ichiti tanunurwa.
Hatina kuziva kupemberera n'anga neinobata mai.
Hezvo, nhasi tave kutanda botso.
Todya nhoko dzezvironda,
Kutambura munyika yokwedu vauyi vachidya rifa.
Wekuchemera zvino tamushaya,
Mazvekudaka aya?
Takazviparira toga.
Kutadza kuri matiri vana venyu,
Samasimba tinzwireiwo ngoni.
Zame tinunureiwo tateterera.

REGRET
Simbarashe Chirikure
Translated by Oscar Gwiriri

Like a calf during a graze
We rejoice and danced like David.
Hoping that we were relieved,
Unaware we were celebrating evil,
Today we're tormented by aggrieved spirits,
Living from hand to mouth,
Suffering in our own country
At the expense of settlers.
There is nobody to talk to,
Isn't it by our own liking?
We have inflicted ourselves,
Of course we sometimes go astray,
But Lord, have mercy upon us!
We have suffered just enough.

KODZERO YANGU
Simbarashe Chirikure

Muri mubereki pasina vabereki,
Mudzidzisi ndimi muchengetedzi wangu.
Vabereki vakaisa chivimbo mamuri,
Chivimbo chekuti muchandipa zivo remabhuku,
Mugondidzidzisa tsika nehunhu zvakanaka,
Muri mucherechedzo wakanaka kwandiri.
Zvino zvamaita izvi manditadzira mudzidzisi.
Pakubata bata muviri wangu matotyora kodzero dzangu.
Iyi nhau ndotoisvitsa kumukuru wechikoro chete.
Naivo vangu vabereki ndotovazivisa chete.
Munofanira kurangwa iyemi mudzidzisi,
Mukaregererwa mungamwauka semucheka waora,
Muchityoredzera kodzero dzevana vanovimba nemi.
Nhasi maigochera pautsi, manyangira yaona,
Bumbiro remutemo wenyika haritendere tsika yenyu iyi.
Matambira kunonyudza, mutemo ngauite basa rawo.

My rights
Simbarashe Chirikure
Translated by Oscar Gwiriri

You are a parental representative,
Oh teacher, my dear keeper!
My parents have bestowed trust in you
With the hope that you'll part knowledge
And guide me to follow a good life path,
Oh teacher, my guardian angel,
But why then, betraying our trust.
Fondling my body is an unwarranted
Violation of my human dignity and rights.
For surely, I will report this to the authorities.
I will relate everything to my trustful parents.
You deserve an authoritative retribution, Sir,
To tame down your vulturistic pedophilia.
You have taken a wrong and costly turn, Sir!
The Constitution and regulations protect us,
Let the law take its course upon you, Sir.

Ndichadiwawo here?
Natasha Tinotenda Gwiriri

Bva, makasarudza ini panyika yose kuti ndiite weropa rejongwe.
Heya makati ini ndini wemunyama nhai?
Mukaongorora moyo yose mukaona wangu uri wedombo .
Makati vehutsinye vatsike nepamusoro pawo, hapana chakashata.
Ko, ini makati handinawo kodzero yekufarawo nhai?
Ho-o, kubva makandiisa kudivi rana murambiwa nhai?
Uyu abata neapa anosema oti tsve, kundisiya kwakadaro.
Ndikati ndawana shamwari yemoyo, yofuratidzwa yoti tsve zvakare.
Haika nhasi ndazodzidza,wangu moyo hauna wawo.
Ko, mungandipindurawo here Nyakusika woye,
Ndichazodiwawo,
Naani zvake iyeye ane tsitsi?
Misodzi iyi ichazooma?
Ko, kunenge kwaitikeiko?
Dai machindinzwa kuchema, mukandinyaradzawo.

Could I be loved?

Natasha Tinotenda Gwiriri
Translated by Oscar Gwiriri

Am I the badly chosen one
Whom you selected as the cruel one
Who deserves this calamity
Upon all the evil trampled on my heart?
Am I not supposed to be happy too?
Ok, you have segregated me as an outcast
Who nauseates whosoever attempts to get closer,
Whoever wants to date me feels repelled.
Now I know, my heart deserves nobody's attention.
But Lord, tell me the truth, O God!
Could I be loved,
By who who has that heart?
Will these tears ever dry?
After how long?
Lord have mercy on me, please!

Ndinokuda
Natasha Tinotenda Gwiriri

Hupenyu hwangu huchinge gomba risina anofutsira,
Kuchema kuriko kudya kwezuva nezuva,
Zuva roga roga misodzi mokoto ndichizvibvunza,
Mibvunzo kuna Mwari ichiti,
Vanombodiwa ndivana ani?
Vanodiwa wani vana vevamwe ?
Vevamwe ndovakaita seiko?
Ko, ini?
Ko, ini ndakaita sei ndisina wangu?
Asi, waiva mubvunzo weasina meso,
Asina meso anoona zviri mberi.
Dai vakanga uripo, ndisina kutambudza nzeve dzaNyakusika.
Zuva iro ravakamazarura masuwo vakandiratidza iwe,
Ndokuvhara buri raipinza mhepo mumoyo mangu,
Misodzi ndokuita chipatapata kudzokera kwayakazarurwa,
Mufaro wakava mutambo mukuru wakafarirwa nemoyo wangu.
Ko, vakati Mwari haasi benzi handiti vakanga vazviona,
Hekani, vakaita zvinoshamisa ndokutisanganisa.
Wakauya ukava makomborero mazhinji kwandiri,
Kubvira pazuva iro Mwari pavakakutuma kwandiri.
Tsinga dzangu dzakasvipa zvimwe dzikasarudza iwe,
Kureva kuti wava hupenyu hwangu narini.
Kubva kwako pandiri, ndobva ndaparara.
Asi, Mwari vangada kuti ndiparare here?
Aiwa kwete!
Naizvozvo ndichava newe kusvika musi wandinosiya nyika.
Ndinokuda ufunge!
Mashoko angu haangatsanangure zvizere.

I love you
Natasha Tinotenda Gwiriri
Translated by Oscar Gwiriri

Whilst my life was like a hell pity,
Mourning being the daily bread,
Tears throbbing as I asked myself
And God about who deserves love.
Some people are loved unconditionally,
What's their difference with me,
What is really wrong with me?
Oh, it was just a silly question
A question by a blindfolded person
Blind not to see what the future holds.
Had you been there, I wouldn't trouble
Heavens with unnecessary queries.
The day my requests were answered
He showed me you my love
And plugged the hole to my hurt heart,
And tears suddenly dried off my cheeks,
Drawing eternal happiness to my soul.
No wonder why it is said He is a loving God,
He has brought you and me together,
And you were a rare gift to the troubled me.
From the day I met you and loved you,
My mind abandoned all my worries
And embraced you as my one and only.
Never leave me darling, or else I'll perish.
But, our loving God will never let us part.
By that, I shall be yours forever till I die.
I Love You!
Words may not express my deepest love for you.

Fiction

THE DEMOLITION
HOSEA TOKWE

The Commuter Bus did not stop at the popular DST Bus Stop but moved on into the City. There were groans and howls as the few passengers who had "P*ass Letters*" complained to the driver. These were the lucky ones to be allowed to board the bus and enter the City during this time of the Coronavirus pandemic outbreak. The bus had stopped at a manned roadblock some two kilometres away and the traffic police were satisfied with the evidence they were shown. Indeed these passengers had genuine reasons to come into the City.

"Where are you going to drop us now huh?"

"Hey stop here!"

"This old man is a deaf idiot" bellowed a bulky man furiously.

But the old metallic bus with its loud deafening engine moved on. The rattling noise from the old engine drowned out all else and some women who were already enjoying the spectacle laughed amid the confusion. Passengers who had left their seats intending to drop off at the popular bus stop stood along the aisle but the bus moved on. Now it was weaving its way through the fast built-up of traffic as workers eager to be at work early competed with each other amid the heavy hustle and bustle.

Jealous, a tall middle aged man, putting on a black cap inscribed "*New York*" on the forehead wore a dejected look on his face and sat pensively by the seat close to the door anxiously watching the aged bus driver dressed in a faded green shirt with threads on seams as he struggled with the handbrakes. Sharp knuckles shown on the driver's right hand and dark thick veins bulged as he summoned all his effort to control the rickety bus that heaved and jerked each time it pulled off as the traffic jam eased.

"I will drop here conductor" announced a middle aged man

"Noooo!" responded the conductor

"You will get me arrested for jumping at a traffic intersection from a moving bus" he shouted with a voice full of anger.

Now he was reminding every passenger that they had travelled very well all the way from the locations and now that they were weaving their way in the city he did not want any trouble with the police. But the passengers were restless shoving each other but he could not allow them take it their way until arrival at the bus rank, the final destination. The passengers were growing restless as the commuter bus was now taking too long to arrive as it negotiated the clogged traffic.

Tired of standing Jealous sat down again and gazed through the window at the old building *"Victory Building 1953"*. This is the building that had been turned into one of the thriving *Nyaningwe Supermarket* in years gone by now. It has been one of the Supermarkets that had accepted multicurrency purchase of goods soon after the formation of the Government of National Unity (GNU) but to imagine it being closed now was difficult to fathom.

Something unusual caught Jealous' eyes. Where were the vendors who by now would have been unzipping their huge sacks of merchandise and laid them on the city pavements? Again he was asking himself why the foreign currency dealers' cars with dark-tainted windows were not at their parking lot. He felt a slight apprehension.

"Tickets tickets tickets please" the smiling conductor extended his arm to receive back half torn tickets. The bus had now arrived at the deserted old rank.

Jealous stood up and stepped into the aisle as he took a breather whilst the other passengers trickled out in single file. Soon he dropped his right foot to the ground he felt some cool air. There was a deadly silence and a cool wind was moaning softly through what used to be a busy and noisy terminus. As it blew from the east it swept some scrap papers in all directions. Jealous found himself wiping away dust from his eyes. The bus rank was deserted and bus sheds were bare and empty. Was he at the right place? At first he could not believe his eyes.

"Hit it hit it" an uproarious bunch of unemployed men urged on.

"Damage it, destroy", bellowed another man

Jealous moved faster urged by the spectacle from the crowd. Men, women and vagrants milled as they cheered wildly at the noisy Cat Demolition Caterpillar vehicle. As he urged closer he could now see its sharp claws twisting and turning in the air as if looking for prey. The driver reversed the monster like Caterpillar and it advanced forward amid wild cheers, its target a lone pillar.

With a forceful strength it hit the pillar. The pillar at first stood its ground shaking sideways buoyed by steel rails that had held the cement for years, but then its resistance would not hold forever and it dropped off heavily leaving a cloud of dust in the air. It was reduced, a heap of rubble.

"What is happening?" Jealous heaved with astonishment.

Nobody answered him at first

"I said what is going on here?" Before he could say out another question a man with dusty hair nudged and cupped his mouth to his ears.

"This is the demolition" he hissed into his ears

"The Municipality is demolishing all illegal shacks that had been erected here at the bus terminus all these years" giggled the man as he watched the crowd cheer again at another falling pillar.

Three weeks in advance word had gone that the Municipal authorities were going to pull down all the sheds and shacks that had sprouted at the popular Kudzanayi Bus Terminus. This terminus had been built before Independence for rural bus operators to pick and drop passengers. With the turn of the century and the economy worsening from 2005-2008 vendors had erected more stalls, some selling their merchandise in the form of nails, hoes, shovels even yokes and fencing wire. From another end where the Omnibus picked up passengers commuting from high density suburbs, where the majority of low income earners lived, vegetable, fruit and tomato stalls soon sprouted alarmingly. Then the small groceries mini-shops mushroomed, here the "poor man's shops" as they became known became very popular selling their basic commodities like cooking oil, sugar, soap and salt in the much detested Zimbabwe bond notes currency. It was said one could get any product in these mini shops. With the sudden emergence of the Coronavirus threat the local city fathers could have none of it. The Mayor of the City of Gweru had been in the news announcing that all these shacks would be destroyed in order to bring back sanity to the City and enforce strict City By-Laws. It had been overheard that some of the Municipal Officers were running clandestine stalls using middlemen to run their illegal informal businesses. This brought more urgency for the speedy destruction of the stalls to avoid prosecution.

Jealous had come into the City of Gweru, the City of Progress so they called it those days. Staying with his Uncle in the high density suburbs Jealous soon applied for an Engineering Certificate Course at the local Polytechnic and commuted daily. Bright, brilliant and intelligent, Jealous was already making plans for his future. With so many industries in the light industrial areas he was certain he would secure a job after finishing his course. Two years had passed and Jealous achieved his dream, a Certificate in Engineering.

"Now what would you like to do now" Jealous' father threw the question which caught him unawares.

"I will get a good job and after a year will plan to further my studies at any University in the country" responded Jealous with a broad smile on his face.

His father now aging, disagreed and advised him to get married for life in the city was not safe for a working young man, he told him. He did not want to disappoint his aging father, so he got married. Back in the City Jealous stayed with his Uncle.

Uncle Jethro was a Municipal Police Sergeant then. His work involved supervising street raids. Despite vendors being allocated stalls others had resorted to laying their wares on street corners beckoning passers-by to buy their wares. This practice annoyed Jealous for at some street corners there was disruption of free movement. Uncle had at one point invited Jealous to apply for a job but he was quick to turn back the advice. To imagine him an Engineering Certificate holder chasing after women vendors was an affront to his qualification. He had even hinted about his uncle's advice to his friend who had secured a University place who quickly advised him against it. But Uncle Jethro had insisted on him getting employed and support his family for going to University he said, would be like signing a death certificate. He alleged that University students had become drug pedlars, misfits of society and of lose morals by cohabiting in University Hostels. He even told him that others had turned into gays and lesbians. Jealous did not give mind to all this talk for his focus remained on furthering his education.

That was two years ago, Jealous as he wore a faded green shirt had realised that all his dreams had been shattered. The economic meltdown came at the turn of the century as Zimbabwe experienced a hyperinflation never seen in the country's history. Left with no option he teamed up with friends secured a passport and found himself travelling and crossing borders into Botswana, a foreign land to buy groceries for resale at home. It worked as Weekend Street Markets were opened. Things worked well for sometime but as things turned everything came to an end. The short-lived experience had taught Jealous a valuable lesson in survival.

The economy never improved. Could he still stay at home and only wait to be fed by his Uncle? No! Jealous shook his head as he remembered when he had managed to buy food for his family, feed his aged father and even clothing his sightless granny. Now each day Jealous would wake up and visit the produce market. He would find the market full of tired and sweating people moving with little effort and speaking in low voices as if to conserve energy. Here and there week long banana leaves and yellow buns could be seen in open baskets where they were now cracking under the cruel sun. Tobacco leaves dangled from strings like dead rats.

The people milling about at the market were drowsy, as though the burning rays had melted their strength and resolution. Even insects, which always fluttered and buzzed about happily in the mornings, the light gleaming brightly on their wings, had now disappeared into the shadows. Life was hush, people were hustling and the bus terminus had been turned into a sprawling marketplace of heterogeneous products. Amid this entire melee, there were basket-weavers and storytellers and petty thieves and brigands in abundance.

Now all this was gone. Jealous had heard his Uncle talk about the demolition, but then the Lockdown was already being enforced.

As he stood visibly disoriented, he could not believe that right where he stood was the exact location where a thriving business was once conducted. He tried in vain to reconstruct in his mind the details of the stall he had owned. Why had he not listened to words doing the rounds about news of the demolitions assuming they were mere rumours. Of course the City Fathers no longer wanted informal traders to do their business in the Central Business District.

Jealous stood there confused. As thoughts raced through his mind, two big teardrops slipped out of his eyes and rolled unheeded down his cheeks. Inside him the world had crashed and his body felt heavy.

"Hey move away, move away" the Municipal Sergeant accompanied by his team had jumped from a pick-up as police details moved a distance away.

"We said we no longer want people, but you keep on coming"

"Move away!!" he shouted angrily

"Go to your rural homes and cultivate crops"

"Don't you have rural homes" another Municipal Policeman mocked

"And you young man! You are an embarrassment standing as if you have nothing to do"

"I said move before I bushwhack you" the Municipal Sergeant warned.

The humiliation that Jealous felt gnawed his heart. The harder he tried to push it to the back of his mind the more it tortured him. He was hurt and the cut was very deep in his soul. His youthful face had become like that of an old wizard approaching his eighties. Weighty considerations now occupied his mind.

The sun rose announcing that soon it would be hot. The demolition continued as the roaring sounds of the Caterpillar deafened the environs. The crowd some fearing arrest soon dispersed one by one. Their feet negotiated their way through rubble, big concrete slabs, contorted metal poles and remnants of broken planks and black plastics that had provided the shed to their wares. Built in the early twentieth century the

106

Rural Terminus was at last gone, Gweru the *City of Progress* had regressed into an abrupt quietude.

As Jealous looked at the demolition for the last time, an overwhelming worm of despair and sense of irredeemable loss wriggled in the very marrow of his bones and was slowly eating him away as he retraced his steps home.

Raki
Takunda Shepherd Chikomo

I'm not saying I'm a lucky bastard but on this particular day I felt like one. That "lucky enough ndapona" Oliver Mtukudzi song since that moment became more than just a song to me, it became an anthem. I found my atonement on this fateful day.

My car is an old piece of metal, being an heirloom it has seen its fair share of near misses. I was taking the final stretch of Chitungwiza road before I took the right turn into Tilcor road, which would be my last stretch of tarred road before the dust one that would lead me straight home.

So I pressed on the gas and pushed the needle up to 120. Even I could feel that the machine was stretching its legs more than it should because it then grew an unusual vibration to it and the engine noise at somewhere around eighty kilometres per hour changed from a hummy groan to a robust grinding noise that made it feel like it was speeding when it wasn't.

Regardless, I pressed on, ignored my wife who by the time I got to 120 had woken up from her travel sleep and I could see by the boogie look in her eyes that these palpitatious bulging of eyes wasn't just her waking up from sleep but she was warning me that I was speeding and had to reduce speed. In my defence I was tired and besides it was the last stretch of road before getting home, what could possibly go wrong? So I hit it even harder.

Of course it was a wide tarred carriageway, I wasn't speeding that much, my car of inheritance was just scared of anything above a hundred, well, I wasn't. Besides I wasn't even going that fast because there were some powerful 21st century beasts that were still being hit where blood oozes such as the Mercedes C220 that passed me and the Prado VX Executive that looked as though they were being driven by some honourable ministers who were rushing to parliament to commit some honourable crime.

Nonetheless, this wasn't reason to hate my 84 Toyota Cressida because it still went fast enough to scare my wife in the front passenger seat, and myself too. Inside lane, approaching at 120 kilometres an hour, came my white Cressida, right indicator now on, I knew it to notoriously fail whenever it pleased so I also made a hand signal, my right hand out, pointing right in an up and down motion, I signalled thrice and began to ease off on the gas. I could hear the two litre diesel engine begin to breath and moan much peacefully as I let go off the gas for the brakes.

Chitungwiza road is intersect with Tilcor road which to the other end then leads to Chitungwiza's once vibrant pride and joy, Tilcor industrial area. Now it's just a ghostly scrapyard where the only sign of life is the tortured Zupco bus company depot and the residential dump site that's cleaner than our houses because the Municipality dare not collect waste anymore. This being the norm in Chitungwiza, we make do without traffic lights. "...drivers are to drive at their own risk and practice safety..." I once heard a VID officer say this to a colleague of his at Makoni VID. Today his words were put to the test.

Flying like the concord, to my left, a car overtook my Cressida in the blink of an eye. It went so fast what was left of it was just the sound of a car that had already passed. It was a grey Volkswagen golf MK7. He took me just as I was taking my right. In the opposite lane there was approaching a white Nissan Tiida that was signalling to turn right, thus was going in my opposite to the Industrial area. This Tiida driver assuming he had evaded danger by avoiding the large pothole that lay proud in the middle of road right by the intersection, nothing in the world was to prepare him for what was going to happen next.

That's when it all happened. The Volkswagen took me as I turned right, the Tiida turned also, so that meant there's no way the driver could have seen the golf coming and also manoeuvre around the pothole in time to successfully evade the golf, so he just made for it. In that moment, tyre screeches sounded so heavy and loud it felt like the car was going to burn them out in that instant. The driver of the golf seeing the Tiida approaching into his lane, dashed to the left, hit his brakes hard and in that instant the world took a chill pill and everything in that one second happened in slow motion.

As the Tiida driver came to his senses in that New Yorkian time he too hit his brakes hard, stopped, held onto his steering wheel for dear life, his mind possibly assuming what could have been the worst because had he stopped half a second late he could have been involved. The grey Golf was still in motion, swerving to the left and then right leaving a trail of dark smoky S's in the tarmac.

What I should mention is that this intersection is also where mini buses from Makoni to Machipisa drop off workers and pick up other passengers, so it's quite a buzz as people and cars play real life Monopoly. The grey car as it tried to evade the Nissan swerved left, where there were a group of workers waiting to hitch a ride back home after a long working day. One man of about his early thirties, he's the one who said, "Mukabika sarai muchidya mega".

The golf picked him up by cutting off both his legs, making him airborne, hit his back hard against the frangible windscreen smashed it inside, got stuck in there as the driver made a dash for the other direction to avoid hitting other people and he just lay there motionless and lifeless. Since his car was moving so fast he couldn't stop in time to avoid an eighteen wheeler Scania truck that was oncoming in the opposite direction. The grey car, with the industrial worker on screen crushed into the truck head-on, blood spilling all over, like raspberry juice. By the roadside people were just standing akimbo mouths open wide, others who had the strength had hands on the back of their heads and some covering their wide open eyes and mouths. Those who had been missed by the swerving car ran for their lives and jumped into the nearby grassy bushes and watched from there. Some later on confessed to wetting their pants.

He smashed right into the haulage truck, and in that moment his car blew up into flames, the fire erupting like the Hiroshima Nagasaki, and the noise there was so intense it surely felt like a bomb had gone off and deafened our ears. Because HGV's are not that quick to stop, the truck dragged with it the grey car, smashed it into the back of the Nissan Tiida which was still by the middle of the road, rolled it over three times and it too caught fire and lit up in flames beyond recognition.

As the truck finally came to a halt, other drivers who had witnessed this carnage, quickly ran to the grey Volkswagen that was glued in the face of the truck and burning and poured fire extinguishing fluid into the face of the fire trying their best to cut it out. When they eventually did, it was too late to have any hopes of saving a soul from the wreckage. The unfortunate industrial worker was charred by the fire, two occupants in the front, including the driver were crushed into their seats, half burnt half butchered by the front bumper of the truck because it smashed right into the windscreen, through the already knocked out man into their half bamboozled limbs and leaving them there just like that. As if they didn't have any life just a few seconds earlier.

The truck driver having suffered severe head injuries couldn't move out of his truck, so I made for the door and made my best to open the stuck door and help him out. Because the door was jammed, I smashed the window, got inside the truck, called for assistance and helped the helpless man out. Meanwhile another man was already making emergency calls to the hospital and fire brigade, because in that moment that's when the truck driver said diesel and pointed out to a large 1203 tank he was carrying behind. It had not occurred to us that his truck was ferrying diesel to a station at Makoni. I recalled earlier passing by the station and there was a long winding queue of cars, buses and trucks alike. Having been made aware of this highly flammable situation, there wasn't any time to waste because the tank had already begun leaking. An alarm was raised and people quickly moved to a safe distance from the scene.

Thirty minutes passed, the grey car had reignited itself, spreading the fire to the head of the truck which in turn ignited the diesel tank that exploded even bigger than had happened earlier. The earth shook with the force of nuclear bombs, causing the women who were by the scene to wail and constipate their faces into what only could be described as a frenzy of cries. Although safe in a distance, the heat was so intense people's faces could be seen sweating in the orange light. The fire guzzled into the sky lighting up the dusky evening as though the sun had lit up the earth the second time, only that this time around the light was more pronounced than a lazy dusky sun about to knock off into its mother's baby pouch.

The fire response team was nowhere in sight, besides their station being a five minute drive from the scene of the accident. I guessed they didn't have water in their fire trucks. The ambulance only came in time to pick up the corpse of the truck driver, they too were true to their promise of showing up…not to save a soul but to carry a dead one, if you're lucky they will carry one alive only for them to be pronounced dead by the time they get to hospital. Chitungwiza general wasn't that far away either, they must have been late because they were waiting for fuel, probably the same fuel that now lit up the night sky.

We just stood there, helpless…

(Raki - a loose direct translation in Shona of the English term lucky).

112

The crusade
Oscar Gwiriri

A Good News Bible was in Chamunorwa's left hand whilst the right one sporadically clenched into fists as if it was activating his mind to concentrate on what was in his thoughts. He felt as if his face was peeling off with the Honde Valley heat.

'The church must do something about upgrading the road to my homestead,' he thought. His imagination of being Jesus toiling up Golgotha kept him going up the hill. He arrived near a kraal and remembered how he used to spend so much time there watching a dung beetle pushing a ball backwards. However, he also recalled and regretted the boyhood games and all the 'wasted years' he lived in the village wrapped in ignorance of true worship. He condemned his past participation in traditional 'devilish' rituals. His pace dropped as he recalled the day elders and his peers laughed at him after failing a masculine exercise at the traditional initiation shrine. He had received the manhood lessons, then on the final tests each of them was tied on the waist with a yoke strap to practice an erotic dance. Thereafter they got circumcised. During that initiation, Chamunorwa released his bowl. The village elders called him a 'woman' and many predicted an ill fate on his reed mat.

Solo who was seated with the elders at the courtyard was not impressed by his cousin Chamunorwa whom the elders were giving a home-coming and merry reception. Their grandmother brought a clay pot of the seven-days-brewed beer, which was due for sale the following day, Saturday. Saturday was an appropriate day for guzzling.

Suddenly, a village juvenile ran into the courtyard panting and shouting, "There are intruders down the valley! Maybe war has started again! Intruders, invaders down there pitching up tents! Tents bigger than this courtyard! Bigger than grandmother's kitchen hut!"

113

"What! Never in my territory! Warriors, check it up then beat up the *Shima* drum to gather the village men if all is not well! Never!" The chief, Solo and Chamunorwa's grandfather fumed.

By then Solo had not yet greeted Chamunorwa who was sitted on a chair which belonged to the chief's aides. A suit swallowed him and a necktie was pulled loose on the neck.

"Take it easy grandpa; I came along with those people. They are under my command." Chamunorwa reassured.

"That's what you should have said first upon your arrival Chamunorwa, lest we harass visitors and disappoint the ancestors."

"I was about to do so grandpa" Chamunorwa defended.

"You children really don't grow. First thing first! Why then did you abandon them down the valley? Your grandmother brewed beer as if she predicted that there would be visitors. Anyway, she should have got the prediction from a bee which was buzzing around her." Grandfather smiled.

"Not really grandpa, they don't drink. They are devoted Christians. Original and genuine!" Chamunorwa emphasised.

"The village is full of church goers. We're Christians too." Grandfather swiveled a beer calabash and continued to say, "We still go for Sunday service at our Holy Cross Manunure Church."

Twang! Twang! Twang! The sharp ringing sound of crashing guitars echoes from the caves, disturbing an interesting conversation. Skeletons of chiefs falling on each other rattled in the nearby sacred Bura caves. Down the valley, a diesel generator groaned, but the groan was gulped by the 1-2-3- testing of the haunting high-output metallic distorted tones of seven-string guitars. Confusion set in as the elders glanced at each other's face searching for an answer for no question. Chamunorwa explained about his arrangement to have a Ministry at the village.

"Whom did you arrange with first of all? Don't you know that you may disappoint the spirits of the soil? You children never learnt enough during your youthhood lessons and practices." Grandfather asked.

Grandfather was angry with all of the youngsters as he was seated over there scrutinising Chamunorwa.

'Chamunorwa is still a mosquito thin. All what he seems to have acquired from the city is the forced dignity and some somewhat new clothes. Oh, ancestors have mercy.' Grandfather thought.

'No matter how Chamunorwa undermines our traditional values, the elders seem to compromise, and above all they are giving him undue respect. But why?" Solo thought.

His rational mind raged again, 'After all, who is he to sit on our chair of authority? Chamunorwa, the mere boy who failed the traditional test and further failed at school, then resolvedly joined the church to compensate his weaknesses? Why is the church treated as a refuge institution by those with social shortcomings?'

Solo's eyes screwed on Chamunorwa's dressing whilst the elders were forging the way forward with the church crusade in the village valley. A lump of saliva choked Solo's throat. He quitted the traditional court session in silent protest.

Solo walked round the village searching for his friends. Nobody was home. Absolutely nobody. Livestock had been already closed behind pens, yet it was not yet eve. The praise and worship down the valley was sweet and luring. Solo swore to himself that he would never go there. 'After all the elders never bothered to consult us as usual as *the future of the village* as they have always promised.' Solo condemned the traditional courtyard discussions. He thought, 'How could Chamunorwa casually greet me as if I had not lost a mother during his absence? Not even a word or face of condolences? I hate him for this cultural misnomer. But how come, not even a lamentation offering' Solo was perplexed.

Solo complained to himself as he was walking down the valley where the arrows of the musical instruments, praise and worship and mourning were escaping through the big tent side folds. Solo trickled on a stump. He was just wandering in the forest nodding his head time and again, pre-occupied with mixed thoughts. He found himself standing just a

115

short distance from the crusade tent. It was demonically big. Big like crocheting acacia branches in the savanna. It had blue and yellow strips. So colourful even in that darkness of the eve. The canvas was rolled quarter way up like a school girl's socks. The tent lights powered by the noisy generator illuminated the black feet underneath the tent. Some were clean and others soiled. Bare little feet were in there too. Wrinkled and cracked thin legs stood still like steel rail poles erected in the ground. He could see shorts, culottes, dungarees, spray-on jeans and cropped pants balancing on high-heeled shoes swaying sideways. Dirt legs were thriving to imitate the modern dances. It was like a crop field infested with weeds.

'I will not enter into that tent. I hate it. My traditional beliefs and culture reservations restrains me. I'm not a cultural extremist of course, but principled.' Solo vowed to himself.

Solo somehow got angry with himself for coming closer to the tent. He involuntarily tapped his leg to the heavy beat and soft melodies, whilst listening to Chamunorwa who was giving preaching bouts. Solo raised his hands and plugged his ears with his forefingers for a while. Total silence and ancient peace surrounded him. He felt the ground cracking with sound. A multitude of feet were stumping it like the devil compressing corpses in a hell oven. The raucous guitars were stashing through the grains of his fingerprints just to pierce his eardrums. He could feel the atmosphere seemingly bewitched. He supposed that all the fresh air was suctioned into the tent leaving nothing for anything outside it. In his eyes he could see aggrieved village ancestral spirits perspired fire in an invasion protest. He felt that the masquerading mosquitoes were also scared of the so-called Chamunorwa's Ministry crusade. He could hear them flying away and bursting in the air. He turned his head and felt that the ancient spirits were threatened by the public address system, and ghosts resurrected from their graves then roamed around the grave yard. Yes, he could see the spectre sparks right before his eyes. He was convinced that something uncultured was happening inside the tent. Something his father never did even during the sacrament at Holy Cross

Manunure Church. He wanted to walk away from that tent, but the music was enchantingly hypnotising. It was rather hysterical and luring.

Solo stood at the corner inside the holy tent. Village children were dancing their hearts out, and swirling sweets had been thrown in the air. Village elders folded their arms at breast level, gazing. Grandfather was just standing there in astonishment like everybody else. The strangers were really rocking. Rocking madly. Praise and worship dominated even the village dogs' barking and owls' hooting. Testimonials time and sermons time came and passed by. The electric band was playing on a rostrum behind Chamunorwa's glass podium. A lead guitar was thrilling and raising Solo's hair when played on its own. There were no benches like at Holy Cross Manunure Church. The praise and worship ladies had their hair strengthened, some curled, and others were in black-eyed songbird's style. They had long stretched short and body tops, which shaped all the contours of their holy bodies.

'Attractive and arousing girls. Chamunorwa must be having a nice time with them I think. Had it been me, with all those beautiful girls? Oh shame, poor Chamunorwa is a 'woman' after all.' Solo thought.

There were a few adult strangers in the tent. They were also dressed like the youths, and above all, they were with the women not putting on head shawls like the village women ought to do. They also sung, shouted and cried in tandem with the hysterical youths. Most of the visiting ladies were dressed like young girls, but seemed to have clocked past the age of marriage like Chamunorwa.

Chamunorwa bellowed his sermon in English whilst stubbornly lodging his left hand in the trousers pocket and his right hand like a madman begging to some berated spirits. Another Brother translated it into standard Zezuru. The villagers were an ancient Manyika tribe, and some of his words did not go down well with them. Foul language some sort of swirled and swelled beneath the tent like a tornado.

Chamunorwa grovelingly broke into song:

Humble ya Salf
Before da Lawdy …

His peers shouted above their souls:

He-will-lift ya up!

Chamunorwa continued, tears trenching down his bony cheeks,

He will lift ya-aaah!

'Tears? Oh, silly boy! Poor Chamunorwa. What a shameful bunch of a foible.' Solo uttered.

Chamunorwa continued and repeated the chorus whilst facing up the tent as if luring for a drop of water from the sky spirits.

He will lift ya up!

The guests were also raising their arms high above their heads imitating everything Chamunorwa was doing.

'Shame! Anyway, it's not bad for a 'woman' to lead other women and stray men.' Solo thought.

The crusaders exploded into prayer. Cried their guts out. They hopped and shouted. Hands clapping and waving became the order of the prayer. Chamunorwa concluded his prayer and his followers automatically halted in a certain fashion. The villagers watched with awe. The Sisters wiped sweat off their powdered brows. The Brothers' shirts were wet with salty sweat. The villagers were perturbed by the revival, compassionate dragging and soulful singing by Chamunorwa and his praise and worship Brothers and Sisters

Blessed assurance, Jizas is mine:
O what a fore taste of glory divine!

Chamunorwa's voice drowned into a horsy and trancing groan. Solo watched his grandfather nodding his head with amazement. The strangers clapped hands as they sang along:

This is my story, this is my song,
Praising my Saviour all the day long.

They repeated and repeated the chorus. A sister's soprano voice kept the song going lowly as Chamunorwa fell into a trance of prayer:

O Lawdy my Gawd! Lawdy my ...aah!
Punish those corrupt ... aah!
No matter judgment is for... aah!
But Gawd can't you see development is lagging in... aah!
Punish'em if you're the real Gawd I... aah!
Cleanse this village of... aah!
Serve them from the vain orthodox worship... aah!

The strangers interjected with exclamations before the completion of each sentence:

Amen! ...Hallelujah!...Say it Bro!... That's it man!
Praise the Lord!... Jizas!... O my God! ... Save him!

Almost every visitor in the tent was closing eyes. Arms flung outwards. The worshippers burst into prayer once again. What a fracas atmosphere before Solo's scrutinising eyes?

The attending villager's in the tent failed to cope up with the pace of events in the beautiful canvas. Chamunorwa called sinners to the front for a collective repentance prayer. None of the villagers even lifted a foot.

'I don't want a 'woman' to set his hands on our sacred people.' Solo thought.

Chamunorwa shouted,
Come ye brothers and sisters!
Lawdy is watching and waiting!
I know this village is full of sinners.
Come! Have courage! Come!

The presumed village sinners stuck their feet on the suffering and trashed grass underneath the tent. All villagers knew that Grandmother Matondindo was a witchcraft queen. She didn't limp to the repentant front post.

'No matter we are lost sheep in the eyes of the crusading guests, we are alright as we are. It is fine being in the same blanket labelled as 'sinners' than having a faction of the righteous and us the 'thickheaded' hosts that will disintegrate our unity as a village people. I like it this way rather.' Solo thought.

"Anyone born of a woman repents every day. Brothers and sisters from Harare, come for prayer," Chamunorwa shouted.

The guests queued up, singing:

O, there is power, power
Wonder-working power!
In the blood of the Lamb!

Chamunorwa set his hand on each guest repentant's forehead, praying briefly. Some repentants spoke in tongues and others fell down as they were prayed on. The public address system was playing, and the keyboard was mesmerising the congregants. Grandfather pulled out his snuff horn, poured a little bit of it on his heel hand, pinched, sniffed and logged some in his mouth. A sing-a-long by the villagers dominated. Crescendo. The strangers were blessed once again.

One of the ladies offered a prayer, "God redeemer my! Surrender thyself unto you Lawd. Gwiriri village this in Lawdy. Bless sinners single souls every of non-repentant village Gawd. Thy shy come unto thee... Blaa...ta.ka.ma...takataka. Bizarre...Gawd" The lady spoke in weird tongues.

The other guests followed suit, speaking in tongues, in that beautiful tent. Stumping of shoes rocked the then bare ground. Cultic shouts and prayers engulfed the colourful tent. Solo watched in confusion. Oh, what a truly enigmatic worship!

The guest crusaders automatically stopped simultaneously to Chamunorwa like a lorry uphill force to an emergency halt.

That lady continued praying, "I know devil you no wait waylay villagers! Devil, take all property mine! Mine husband and everything, but my Jizus no! Gave me Jizus! Gave me Jizus! Gave me Jizus!"

120

The crusade swallowed the whole night. For surely, time is like dew under a leaf. The cocks crowed. A second and third cock crow followed suit.

Chamunorwa lined another prayer session, "Oh Lawdy, Gawdy my mercy! No matter my people can't repent, I will not deny you! Three times the cock has crowed, and I am steadfast, awake doing your work Lawdy. I can't deny like Jonah, this village is Nineveh. It's Israel, Sodom and Gomorrah. O, Lawdy... Gawdy....Gawdy! Rama...tapa..tipa...tapa!"

No matter the singers looked tired and sleepy, the instrumentalists kept on banging. A few Sisters still jingled their tambourines. Some villagers inclusive of Solo had missed their dinner. The strangers had their food packs behind the tent and they took turns to feed. The crusade embraced dawn and rewound with a dolce song:

Awake, my soul, and with the sun
Thy daily stage of duty run....
To pay thy morning sacrifice...

Solo also hummed to the tune. A Brother was walking around with a small artificial reed woven basket to collect offerings from the congregation. The villagers had no money anyway. One of them picked a pebble and placed in that basket. The Brother collected offerings from the strangers. The rays of the sun beamed on their feet.

Some strangers started packing bags, cutlery and instruments into their lorry. They left the keyboard player concluding the rejoicing. Chamunorwa once again called sinners to the repentant's post. Nobody turned up. His peers were then too busy packing up equipment.

Chamunorwa instructed the village youths to assist by picking up litter right round the place. Grandmother Matondindo approached him over what his peers had done when they arrived.

She complained, "Your girls climbed up my peach tree and they harvested all the fruits without my permission."

"Grandma, God created Eden. He did not give ownership of nature to individuals. God will provide and bless the tree with much more fruits during the next season. Believe me" Chamunorwa advised.

As the village youths were picking litter, one of the Brothers conversed with Solo.

"I am Chamunorwa's cousin brother." Solo told the Brother.

"You're blessed bro. Bro Chamunorwa is great, man! Blessed are you!" The Brother praised.

Solo felt honoured. Somehow, he began to like Chamunorwa. That Brother stood starring and admiring Solo as he kept himself busy picking empty food packs which were gathered at the corner of the tent.

"Throw that away! Drop it! Eish!" The Brother shouted pointing to the heap of rubbish grasped in Solo's hand.

"What did you say Brother?" Solo was lost.

The Brother looked aside. He never faced at Solo again.

"Drop that *Heart of a Man* pamphlet! There is a used condom in it!" He whispered to Solo.

"Used condom? I don't understand what you are talking about." Solo whispered back. He started separating the rubbish from his left hand with his right hand, throwing it one by one onto the ground so as to check what was all about the condom. Solo seemed he had never heard about it. The crusaders packed their stuff, and off they went back to the city.

'I will come back again. This time everyone must repent, voluntarily or by force' Chamunorwa thought.

The Big Boys' Club
Mildred Mutize

As usual, the gallery in High Court Number One where Judge Rickson Banga was presiding over the murder trial of Doctor Maxwell Pasi was fully packed. No one wanted to miss the reading of the final judgment that afternoon. Those who could not secure seats in the gallery resorted to TV screens and computers as the trial was being streamed live on broadcast. Everyone in the country hoped that the murderer will be given the harshest sentence for murdering a government minister in cold blood. What made people so furious was that Doctor Max, as he was affectionately known, was admitting to the charge yet proffering neither defence nor excuse for his heinous act. It was as if he had killed the minister for the love of it!

But as Judge Banga was about to begin reading out his carefully crafted judgment, something out of the ordinary had happened. There had been a caller on the telephone line who wished to be heard in the court immediately as his life depended on it. Everything he had learned in law school and in all the years he had been in this field told him that this was not possible, a witness had to appear physically in court and had to be sworn in. But as he opened his mouth, Judge Banga surprised everyone when he told the court orderly to put the call through. If the evidence was as inept as he suspected, he could as well choose to dismiss it, but he reasoned that there was no harm in listening to it. What came out through the external speakers had everyone completely stunned.

"I can say this is so mind blasting!" Judge Banga said when he finally found his voice. "Before making my judgment, I'll have to hear from both sides, state council?" he sighed, then sat back as the Public Prosecutor rose to his feet. He was a heavy looking fellow, slow in speech yet meticulous to detail.

"Your honour, this telephone conversation is a hoax meant to confuse the court and delay justice from being served. First of all, this witness has not been sworn in and if his life is actually in danger, he should have called the police and not this honourable court. Allow me to take you to the case of….."

The prosecutor rambled on but none of what he was saying reached to Judge Banga's mind. His senses were in turmoil. *They will kill me!* He thought wildly. The sharp contrast struck to him, of that time, five years ago when he had been the talk of the nation, when songs of praise had been sung for him. *It's the reason for my predicament now*, his mind told him as it glided back to that time.

The police officers in town had received numerous tip-offs over a new illegal drug which had invaded the streets and was being traded in secrecy. Fact had it that it was being manufactured in Kalibu, a country to the far north and was commonly known as the booster. The drug propelled and increased the number of neurons inside the brain cells, making people more intelligent, shrewder. If taken to excess, however, the neurons will keep on multiplying, forming lumps within brain cells leading to brain tumour. Quiet sadly, the drug had found a rampant and viable market in secondary schools, tertiary colleges and universities as many young students saw it as a catalyst to effective learning.

What perplexed the police was that of all the peddlers they managed to arrest on suspicions of supplying the booster, none among them budged any information regarding the source of the drug or the master minds behind it. What they only achieved to realise was the shocking truth that some primary school children were also now being sucked into the abyss. There was a sudden nationwide outcry as concerned teachers and parents demonstrated to the government for something to be done. But no matter the strategies the police employed, they could not crack the drug source within the country. All they knew was that it was manufactured in the Republic of Kalibu. Security at all the borders and airports had been triple tightened to guard against its smuggling into the country but still the peddling continued and hospitals became swamped with teenagers suffering from tumours.

One day, a suspect was nabbed at a local college gate by the intelligence police for drug peddling and was brought to court. Like many before him, he readily confessed to dealing with drugs but refused to reveal his source. Rickson Banga, a Public Prosecutor by then, after perusing the docket had asked the cops to let him talk to the accused. Naison Ndlovu was tall and lanky, with stained teeth and a foul breath.

There was an air of stubbornness around him.

Banga said, "Naison, it pains me to think you are going to spend the next twenty years in prison."

Naison guffawed insolently. "I'm prepared to go to jail for what I did."

Banga closed the docket and threw it aside. "Why am I even wasting my time? Of course you won't get convicted. The guys you work for will come and pay off the magistrate."

"They won't...!" He realised his mistake but it was too late.

A few minutes later, Banga was on the phone with the Officer in Charge Central Police Station. He gave him three names. Naison was now a key state witness, placed in a safe house with state security.

A week later, Ambassador Bothius Mare was recalled from the Republic of Kalibu where he had been assigned for the past ten years. He was arrested at the airport upon his arrival. He joined in the police cells, two well-known business tycoons, Regis Muto and Leeroy Mucha. They were being jointly charged of several counts under the Dangerous Drugs Act. The trio admitted to the charges. Their trial kicked off two days later with Prosecutor Banga leading the state's case. In the end, the three were found guilty and each sentenced to life imprisonment.

The news of the successful conviction of the leaders of the drug syndicate broke out and spread like a veld fire. The newspapers, broadcasts and social media were awash with the story and Prosecutor Rickson Banga was at the epic centre of praise. If Banga felt elated by the glory and applause on social media, a single phone call two days after the conviction brought him into euphoria.

"That was a job well done, Banga. You made us proud," the Area Prosecutor said.

"Thank you, madam." Banga grinned. Their boss was an iron lady who castigated more than she praised.

"The Governor called me," she went straight to the point. "He said he was impressed by your work and would like to see you this afternoon at his office. 2:15 sharp."

It was just unbelievable.

Banga was surprised by the faces he saw around the gold coated conference table in the grand office. The Governor, Joseph Gano introduced Banga to the men around. Banga was in the seventh sky as he shook hands with prominent men who, up to now he had only seen on television screens and newspapers. There were two government officials, three popular lawyers, about two Radio DJs, and a CEO of a giant company. Everyone in the room was well known in the country.

"Sit down, dear," Gano said. "You must be a real genius to be able to crack that one." All the men nodded.

"Thank you, sir. I was only doing my job." Banga said as he sat down.

"Your record as a senior prosecutor is very remarkable and hard workers should be rewarded. I've great news for you. The Prime Minister has appointed you judge of the High Court. Congratulations, Judge Rickson Banga!" They all clapped hands laughing gaily at Banga's surprised look.

One of the men handed Banga a card. "Here is your membership to the Big Boys' Club, where only important people meet and discuss crucial issues. You are now a member of the Club, Ricky! And one other thing, we are all boys here and we call each other by first name."

"And I'll be in charge of all your financial needs," Freddy, the CEO added. "Anything at all you want; a car, a house, you name it. A judge should be a cut above the rest."

Banga thought he would burst with joy. He felt like a young boy on his birthday, heaped present after present. If he had known the actual conversation between the Governor and the Prime Minister pertaining his promotion, he would have been more thankful to Gano. The Prime Minister had expressed shock when the Governor asked him to appoint Prosecutor Banga to a judge.

"Are you out of your mind, Governor!? Where on earth have you heard of a green eared prosecutor suddenly waking up as a High Court Judge?"

"Banga is not green eared, Sir. Just think of the good work he has done in solving that drug fiasco which has been giving us a headache. Surely promoting him to a judge is the least way we can show him our appreciation."

It had taken the Governor two other phone calls and a dinner with the Prime Minister before he reluctantly gave in to the request.

From that day, Banga's life changed for the better. After being sworn in, he was transferred to the High Court where he spent the first few months sitting in with other judges. He was a hard worker by nature and his in-depth knowledge of the law made him a resourceful person to fellow jury members and his superiors. In the legal circles there was a saying that a good law officer is not the one who knows the law but the one who knows where to find the law. Banga knew both and he was revered by many. In the evenings, he would hang out with the 'Boys' at the Club. Through the Big Boys' Club, Banga was now an acquaintance of the prosperous and important people in the country. All Club members were paid a handsome figure on weekly basis. They had standards to maintain, he had been told. His own standards had also risen and everywhere he went, people always turned to stare.

Banga had been a high court judge for five years when one day, he received an invitation to a formal dinner at a local hotel. As usual, he found himself rubbing shoulders with the VVIP who included foreign dignitaries, government ministers, and business tycoons, among others. Although the ambiance was formal and reserved, Banga could detect a degree of casualness among the guests who were so at ease with one another. He revelled in the fact that he was part of them.

"Got a minute, Ricky?" Gano was beside him, a glass of whiskey in hand. He led Banga out of the drawing room into a smaller office where the Boys were chatting idly, taking sips from their glasses. Gano closed the door as Banga exchanged casual greetings with the Boys before proceeding to the drinks corner. He poured himself a glass of whisky.

"You know, Ricky, you are doing us proud," Gano said behind him. "We like the way you preside over major cases."

"Thanks, Joe," Banga said, turning to him. The boys had all ceased their conversations and had come to stand in an arch behind Gano, facing Banga.

"We think it's high time you start the real work," Gano continued solemnly. "But of course ours won't be complicated. We have got a system where we grill our guys so that whoever is caught admits to all charges and never say a word on who is behind."

For a moment Banga was stupefied. "I...I don't understand."

Gano moved closer to him. "Look here, Ricky. We have got a business to protect. The proceeds are what take care of all of us in the Club. You see, that drug plant in Kalibu where the booster is manufactured is my brain child and the Club's cash cow. We have a large empire working under us that's why we are so rich."

Banga could see that all the Boys were eying him warily, watching closely his reaction. In that instant of deep shock, Banga saw something in the Boys that he had never seen in all these past years. Beneath the glamour they exuded, there was a deep lining of danger and it was surfacing now. He took a timid sip from his glass and when he looked up, a huge grin covered his whole face. "Why did you guys wait this long to tell me? This is very exciting!" The Boys suddenly relaxed.

Gano looked happy. "I was telling the boys you won't give us any problems and they were doubtful. Do you know you were my project from the start? I'm glad you came out fine."

"Your project?"

Gano nodded. "Remember that time you made our peddler reveal some names to you? You gave us quite a fright then. We had two options; either to get rid of you and continue with our operations or to suspend our operations briefly and make you part of us for future use. All the boys voted for the former but I had a hope in you and how right I was! You are now mature enough to know the Club secrets. Peter, you can tell him about the drug fiasco."

Peter, a medical doctor said, "When we resumed our operations in this country last year, the borders were now too risky. We organised that the booster come in along with our country's medical drugs, so that no one suspect them. But things went wrong yesterday when our consignment arrived at the hospital's warehouse. I took along our peddlers to help with their conveyance to our place but as we were loading the truck, Doctor Maxwell Pasi, the Hospital Administrator arrived. Someone should have tipped him off and he in turn called the Minister and told him. He blocked our way and told us to wait until the minister arrives with the police. We immediately attacked him and he fell unconscious. I had to call Joe and he quickly organised someone to get to the minister fast before he spilled the beans."

Gano laughed and said, "You see, Ricky, our guy did an excellent job on the Minister last night and just so that the murder is not linked to our man, Doctor Max will claim responsibility. We pulled him through our processes and he came out fine, just like the rest before him. He is going to be arrested and he will admit to the murder charge." Gano placed a hand on Banga's shoulder and a cold, hard malice flashed in his eyes as he said quietly, "You are going to try him, Ricky. I'll see to it that you do and you shall give him a death penalty." As Banga nodded, Gano had turned to Tasara, from the national broadcast. "I want the trial to be aired live. People would be interested to know that Doctor Max killed a government minister and whilst everyone is glued to the trial, we will smuggle in more drugs."

A week later, Doctor Max's trial had come to an end. That afternoon at 3:30, Judge Banga was going to read out the final judgment and sentence. At 2:45pm, Banga was knocking on the Judge President's chambers. He spent the next forty-five minutes with his boss, talking in confidence. When he finally got out, he headed straight to his courtroom, where everyone was waiting for him.

After the strange call which had everyone in the courtroom dumbfound, the Prosecutor had indeed taken his time, trying to persuade the court to disregard such evidence as there was a high chance of manipulation. When he finally took his seat, the Defence Attorney rose up and bowed low to the Judge. "Your Honour, I have nothing to say. I pray that you follow your instincts in this matter." And he sat down. Everyone was taken aback by this.

After a while, Judge Banga cleared his throat. "After having heard from both sides, I carefully weighed the odds and it is now apparent there is more to this case. I am now releasing Doctor Maxwell Pasi so that the police can make further investigations to this case." He pounded his gavel on the table, symbolising the end of the court session.

As the gallery stood up in anticipation of the Judge's departure, Banga raised a finger at the IT and media personnel who quickly folded their cameras and ran out of the courtroom. At that same moment, four uniformed police officers bowed at the door as they entered the court room. "Good afternoon, your Honour, we are here to offer you state protection."

In the Judge President's chambers the cameras were being quickly set. After a few seconds, Judge President Michael Dorgan was addressing the nation live on air. "Ladies and gentlemen, the situation has taken another twist. I would like to assure you that I've got the blessing of our government to say this on air as it concern the security of our country. This is about a very daring and dangerous drug syndicate which call itself the Big Boys' Club. As we speak the police have them under arrest. Let me start from the beginning...."

Visual art

The Chegutu Bus *by Kudakwashe K Nhevera*

The Chegutu Bus Station painting, commonly known as *Taurai*, is an artistic interpretation of beginnings. For every tree to grow and blossom it must have roots. These are my roots, the life I knew and grew from.

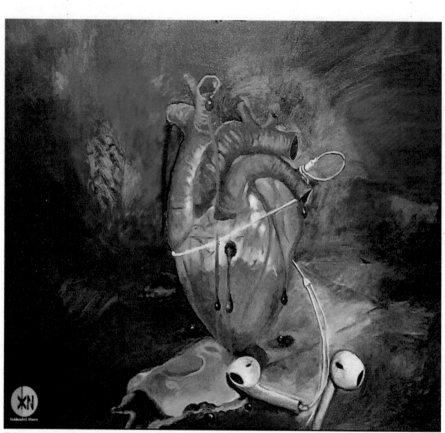

Listen to your Heart *by Kudakwashe K Nhevera*

Listen to your Heart talks of how we as a society get lost in the motions of life and forget what is important which is to listen to our hearts, emotions and inner selves. This is just a gentle reminder to never forget to take time to care for ourselves and listen to our hearts.

Rider *by Kudakwashe K Nhevera*

Dust is a sign of life. In the *Rider* painting this is depicted by the captured essence of an adrenaline rush represented by the biker and his bike that leave behind a cloud of dust. Without activity the dust settles.

Chinyamusaka Gap *by Tendai Rinos Mwanaka*
Photography
December 2015, Zimbabwe, Nyanga, Manicaland Province
Chinyamusaka Gap
I took this photo of the gap between the Nyanga Range of mountains to
the left, and Muchena range of mountains to the right, between them the
land almost flatens, you see for forever. This is one gap in which you can
see so far your sight in the Nyatate valley. The whole eastern side is
totally blocked by the Nyanga range, the north by Muchena range, the
south are Nyahukwe, Turo and Ziwa Mountains, and the biggest part of
the west by Ruchera mountains, so that when you are inside the Nyatate

135

valley there are a few open spaces where your eyesight doesn't get blocked, and this Chinyamusaka gap is one of these. I have written about this gap before in several writings as it used to appear in a lot of folkloric and strange stories I heard growing up. So I grew up sort of fascinated by this gap. But I took it as it represented some door of some sort for us, an opening into another world. It is a frontier an artist gets into, or travels into to find some other forms of fantasy and reality. I have written about doors before, in the collection of essays, *Zimbabwe: The Blame Game*, "It might be the door to the outside, to the backyard lawn, beautiful garden, and beautiful pool. It might be the door to another door, further ahead, and the idea of opening one door after another and another...it is a perpetuating feeling. It might be a door you may never be able to open. It might be a locked door. It might require breaking into. This defeats the whole image of a door. It lets that which is behind the door to take another form, posture, to disappear, to ruffle things a little, and to even change them. It is a door. It might be a door into the very insides of things, feelings, lives, worlds; worlds that are so far into the realms beyond the scribble of this pen. This journey, into doors, the path to; it takes or asks for more, much more." A few lines later I said, "Ideas are like doors, are another thing that amazes me. They open up like doors. You have to open them, pursue them, and own them, if you can. The more you pursue them, the more you get deeper and deeper into their mysteries, their meaning worlds. The worlds of ideas can be a soft or stubborn take." Fascinated by the simple beauty of life and the place, I wrote in another essay, *Nyanga, December 2015: In Search of Ancient Ways,* "The villages nestles quietly below the mountains, goats bleating, scrounging for tree leaves, people walking from the church back to their homes, the thatched huts, the asbestos roofed houses, the cattle kraals, the constant hum of voices, bird calls, the distant laughter, the sun in the skies, a beautiful summer sky, blue. This is a beautiful place, and it's easier to take it for granted if you stay in this place

The Seat of Government by *Tendai Rinos Mwanaka*
Experimental photography
July 2013, Mapfurira Village, Nyatate, Nyanga Zimbabwe
The Seat of Government

I have always been interested in the massive baobab trees of my rural home, Nyatate. There are literary thousands of these trees and they have created, over the years, beautiful shapes we never took time to appreciate. This is one photographic documentary I am itching to do, photographing all these baobab trees. If I get the chance I am going to take it as I know it will be worthwhile. This need to photograph the baobab trees was inspired by this pic of the baobab you see above. This baobab is older than me, it has always been there since I started being aware of my existence in this village of ours. It is pretty much in the middle of the village, and it is used as the meeting point of the village when they have meetings, when they need to decide anything, when they want to apply traditional law to any wrongdoers, so it is our seat of government. It's known as the *Baobab of Mapfurira*. It has grown to dominate the place around it, not just as a seat of government but literary or physically. Its roots are all over that little place, we sit on its roots as our chairs in our House of Lords, or White House or Judiciary. Like this baobab tree dominates the spaces around it, maybe I am encouraging you to dominate the spaces around yourself too, not just by expanding but on a subconscious level, like what this baobab tree do to the Mapfurira villagers. Whilst in the original photo and even this one we see how the trunk, branches, and roots dominate its surrounding, by juxtaposing the same photo of it against it I have created a sense of double domination, as we see a reflection of the baobab propagating this idea of domination, and also I used the computer paint tool to paint a bit of the sky above it, a deep colour that arcs across the sky above it, thus I am alluding to its extending domination into the atmospheres.

The Gallery Wall Space by Tendai Rinos Mwanaka
Watercolours
2015

The Gallery Wall Space is a depiction of the gallery wall with the 3 paintings hung on its three walls, and the unoccupied stool…I invite you to sit on the stool and enjoy the paintings and interpret them whichever way you want to

Mindscape by *Tendai Rinos Mwanaka*
Computer graphics
2012

Mindscape needs no explanation. I used the computer paint tool to create this piece, of the whirls and interconnectivity of the brain that creates a mindscape...a beautiful mindscape

Art by Tendai Rinos Mwanaka
Installation
2016

Art...this doesn't need much explanation too. I decided to utilise junk, used plastic boittles, to create art with; practising recycling, environmental activism and art together!

Mmap Multi-disciplinary Series

If you have enjoyed **Zimbolicious Anthology Vol 5** consider these other fine books in the *Multi-disciplinary Series* from **Mwanaka Media and Publishing:**

Africanization and Americanization Anthology Volume 1, Searching for Interracial, Interstitial, Intersectional and Interstates Meeting Spaces, Africa Vs North America by Tendai R Mwanaka
A Conversation…, A Contact by Tendai Rinos Mwanaka
Africa, UK and Ireland: Writing Politics and Knowledge Production Vol 1 by Tendai R Mwanaka
Writing Language, Culture and Development, Africa Vs Asia Vol 1 by Tendai R Mwanaka, Wanjohi wa Makokha and Upal Deb
Zimbolicious: An Anthology of Zimbabwean Literature and Arts, Vol 3 by Tendai Mwanaka
Drawing Without Licence by Tendai R Mwanaka
Writing Grandmothers/ Escribiendo sobre nuestras raíces: Africa Vs Latin America Vol 2 by Tendai R Mwanaka and Felix Rodriguez
Tiny Human Protection Agency by Megan Landman
Ghetto Symphony by Mandla Mavolwane
A Portrait of Defiance by Tendai Rinos Mwanaka
Nationalism: (Mis)Understanding   Donald Trump's Capitalism, Racism, Global Politics, International Trade and Media Wars, Africa Vs North America Vol 2 by Tendai R Mwanaka
Ouafa and Thawra: About a Lover From Tunisia by Arturo Desimone
Zimbolicious: An Anthology of Zimbabwean Literature and Arts, Vol 4 by Tendai Mwanaka and Jabulani Mzinyathi
Chitungwiza Mushamukuru Anthology by Tendai Mwanaka

Soon to be released

The Day and the Dweller: A Study of the Emerald Tablets by Jonathan Thompson

142

Writing Robotics, Africa Vs Asia, Vol 2 by Tendai Mwanaka and Tembi
Charles

https://facebook.com/MwanakaMediaAndPublishing/